Praise for *The Bully's Trap*

"I have worked with Andrew Faas for a number of years and what he advocates in *The Bully's Trap* is something he has effectively put into practice, particularly in building positive, high performance cultures."

—Glenn Murphy, Former Chair, CEO, Gap Inc.

"In this book, *The Bully's Trap*, Andrew Faas takes bullying in the workplace as an issue that has long been relegated to human resources and powerfully and convincingly makes the assertion that this must be dealt with at the top."

—F. Ross Johnson, former CEO, RJR Nabisco

"*The Bully's Trap* provides an incredible insight on how corporate cultures influence behaviors. Andrew Faas is a voice of reason on this very real issue and this book should be required reading for anyone in management and included in the curriculum for business programs at colleges and universities."

—Paris Vlahovic University of Toronto Graduate Rotman Commerce program, Specialist in Finance and Economics, graduated in 2012

"Andrew Faas in *The Bully's Trap* has really captured what goes on in the workplace. My regret is that I did not have the benefit of his guidance and advice when I was targeted—had I read the book then, I would have handled it in a better way which would have led to a better outcome."

—Catherine Labrosse, Registered Nurse, Ontario, Canada

The Bully's Trap

The Bully's Trap

Bullying in the Workplace
Second Edition

ANDREW FAAS

TATE PUBLISHING
AND ENTERPRISES, LLC

Proceeds from the sale of this book will go to the Faas Foundation www.faasfoundation.com and will be directed to raise awareness on the topic of bullying in the workplace, and provide support to those who are targeted. In October of 2014 the Faas Foundation pledged a one million dollar grant to the Center For Addiction and Mental Health (CAMH) to create the 'Well @ Work' program which will become Canada's most comprehensive, evidence-based service and resource for the promotion and protection of mental health in the workplace. The program will empower workers and help employers create psychologically safe and healthy environments.

In the stories I tell, some names and identifying details have been changed to protect the privacy of individuals and organizations.

The opinions expressed by the author are not necessarily those of Tate Publishing, LLC.

Published by Tate Publishing & Enterprises, LLC
127 E. Trade Center Terrace | Mustang, Oklahoma 73064 USA
1.888.361.9473 | www.tatepublishing.com

Tate Publishing is committed to excellence in the publishing industry. The company reflects the philosophy established by the founders, based on Psalm 68:11,
"The Lord gave the word and great was the company of those who published it."

Published in the United States of America
ISBN: 978-1-62563-483-2
1. Business & Economics / Business Ethics
2. Business & Economics / Business Etiquette
15.05.11

"The workplace is the most dangerous place to be in America."

—US Department of Justice (Grimme)

This book is dedicated to Rollie

"New Research finds that 'man's best friend' could be life savers for veterans of the wars in Iraq and Afghanistan"
—Chris Colin Smithsonian Magazine 2012

Rollie, a magnificent, grey, regal Weimaraner with the saddest green eyes, was my constant companion during the time I was bullied and for the duration of writing this book.

Rollie was my first dog. I adopted him when he was a sixteen-month old puppy, suffering from acute separation anguish, who as a result was the neediest dog I ever encountered. This was okay by me as he gave so much more than he needed. I soon discovered what it really meant to be needed and as he was dependent on me, I was dependent on him.

As a first-time author I went through periods of writers block, self doubt to properly convey the message and extreme frustration with the technology I was using (at one point over four thousand words evaporated into cyberspace!). Rollie was there with me through it all, and although he could not say the words, his eyes conveyed, "Don't worry, Daddy—you can do it." Much of what was written was thought through on my daily two- to three-hour walks with Rollie. He never tired of me talking (I think out loud).

Because I was bullied, for all too long a period I was depressed, angry and my level of confidence fell. Somehow like magic Rollie lifted all of this negative energy—just watching his butt and tail wag on our long walks, his joy when I came home, his constant need to be close and his unwavering trust in me gave me such happiness. There is no question he helped me survive a horrific time, and in the process made me a better person.

On December 2, 2012, at seven years old, Rollie passed away in my arms—looking at me with those sad, trusting eyes until I gently closed them.

Table of Contents

Part Two—The Dynamics of Bullying

Introduction

"Workplace bullying is kind of a new concept;
it's like sexual harassment before Anita Hill...One of the
biggest problems is that it is under the radar."

—Catherine Mattice (Petrecca 2010)

B ased on research I have done, I assert that bullying in the workplace is one of the biggest societal and economic issues we face. It is also the least understood, including how it is defined.

Working in an environment that is free and safe from violence is a fundamental right—the fact is, all too many employees are being denied this right. These people deserve the highest level of protection.

My hope is that through this book, many will share my passion and, when appropriate, become employee activists to force the cultural transformations.

"Why do bullies bully?" The simple answer is because they work in an environment where it is allowed, condoned, encouraged, and even expected.

This is the basic premise of the book: where bullying is not allowed or condoned it will stop.

For bullying to stop, it requires much more than legislation or human resource policies and procedures, it requires a cultural transformation, and everyone has a role to play in this.

I assert that with these transformations, not only will the bullying stop, the performance of individuals and organizations will dramatically improve.

The purpose of this book is not only to draw attention to what has become endemic in the workforce, but to propose comprehensive solutions. Here I draw not only on my own considerable experience, but on the experience of others who have spoken to me in the course of writing this book.

Many have asked—as you, the reader, should—"What makes you an expert on bullying in the workplace?" While I don't view myself as an expert, I do have extensive knowledge on the topic and firsthand experience.

My experience includes:

- over thirty years as a senior executive who has handled numerous bullying situations

- a background in labor relations and human resources

- early in my career being called out for being a bully

- being a bystander, witness, defender and resistor in numerous bullying situations

- having interviewed hundreds of people on the topic during the course of writing this book—and

- being retaliated against for being a whistleblower

Throughout my career I have coached numerous members of the gay and lesbian community on being discriminated against and bullied because of their sexual orientation. I have been fortunate in that, other than a few bigoted comments, I was not discriminated against or targeted as a result of my sexual orientation, but all too many of my friends and associates have been, and I hope that my support and coaching was helpful to them.

I have also mentored a number of women, helping them break through the "glass ceiling"—also cautioning them against the pressure to show their toughness by becoming bullies to get ahead.

To augment my experience and knowledge on the topic, extensive research was conducted.

Again, all of this does not necessarily make me an expert, but I think it qualifies me to make certain assertions and observations and offer viewpoints, guidance, advice and conclusions. More importantly, through all of this I have developed a passion to do what I can to bring the topic out from under the radar so that bullying is stopped and prevented.

The issue of the bullying of children and adolescents in schools has received considerable exposure, largely due to the incidences of suicide where bullying is a factor. There is relatively little published material on workplace bullying that raises the level of awareness, discusses the impact, and provides practical guidelines on how to effectively deal with and stop it. This, then, is the goal of this book.

Also through this book, my desire is to increase the awareness of what constitutes bullying and the risks and the costs of bullying to the individual, the family unit, the organization, and the community.

In this book I challenge those who work in toxic cultures to become witnesses, defenders, and activists, never having to say with regret:

- I could have prevented the ruin of my coworker's career.
- I could have prevented the breakup of a family unit.
- I could have helped avoid the demise of an organization.
- I could have prevented a suicide or attempted suicide.
- I could have prevented someone going postal and killing others.

You will note that I have not focused much on rehabilitating the bully. Many believe that bullying is a learned behavior and can be unlearned. This may be true, however I question the efficacy of stopping the bullying through conflict-resolution techniques, sending bullies to charm school, anger management programs, or diversity and sensitivity seminars. (These are usual methods human resource people employ when they are forced to deal with a bully.)

While it is essential that organizations deal with bullying situations as they occur, it is important to understand that they are usually not isolated but are part of a cultural dynamic, so to prevent and eliminate bullying, I assert the following:

1. A fundamental shift in the attitudes of organizational leaders needs to take place where bullying is viewed as a risk to the individual and to the organization.

2. Policies, procedures and practices on bullying need to go beyond the rhetoric and optics, and need to be applied and enforced. Simply overlaying policies on a culture that condones abusive behavior is not sufficient.

3. Boards of Directors must monitor and audit cultural indicators.

4. If the CEO is the CBO (Chief Bullying Officer) the CEO must either change or be changed.

5. Organizational cultures require transformations which eliminate the fear factor.

6. The organizational response to bullying situations requires that the target and/or whistleblower does not become the villain.

7. The implementation of a performance management system that establishes clear and reasonable expectations and goals that do not pit employees against each other.

8. An employee index needs to become a major component on how managers are measured.

9. A "Red Flag" indicator system is required, which shows warning signals where an employee could be a danger to himself or others.

10. Bullies need to be held accountable for their behaviors and actions.

11. Where workplace bullying is a factor in a suicide, the organization and the bully should face criminal charges.

12. Where workplace bullying causes major harm the organization and the bully should face civil charges.

During the course of writing this book, almost everyone I spoke with about the topic had a story about their own experience or that of someone close to them (friend or family member). Over 300 individuals were interviewed over a four-year period.

Throughout the book I use some of the stories I heard. These stories will put into context what I describe in the book, particularly organizational cultural dynamics and politics, the ways and means of bullying and the devastating impact that bullying can have.

The people I have worked with or interviewed are from across Canada and the United States. They represent a cross section of sectors, private and public, not for profit, governments, manufacturing, retail, health care, resources, transportation and financial services.

All of the interviews were unstructured. I just let them talk, relaying their experiences and those of their family member, friend, or coworker. Rarely did I have to interject to seek clarification. For almost everyone the experience is still fresh in their minds, because they keep reliving it. For many, to be able to talk about it brought some degree of closure.

In listening to their stories I tried to capture what people who are bullied go through under the following categories:

- Reason for being bullied
- Ways and means of bullying
- Reporting

- Organizational response
- Coping and/or reacting
- Impact on: physical and mental health, family, friends, employment
- Roles that bystanders play
- Post bullying outcomes

I do not claim this to be a scientific study; however, what I heard was consistent with research that had been done on the topic. The following outlines the dynamics and the impacts that were expressed.

- In 74 percent of the cases, the bullying was boss to subordinate.
- The main reason people were targeted was to force them out of the organization.
- Most of the targets got caught in what I refer to as *"The Bully's Trap."*
- Almost three-quarters of the cases involved psychological bullying (which was often a mix of verbal and psychological combined), just over half were verbal harassment, and a few were physical.
- In over 66 percent of the cases threats were made, usually related to being let go or demoted.
- Just under half left the organization because of the bullying.
- Those who left had great difficulty in getting re-established.
- Just under a quarter would be considered sexual harassment, covered by statutes. More sexual, sexist, and gender discrimination was reported that did not rise to the level of legally defined sexual harassment.

- Almost all of the targets tried to deal with the situation alone, tended to make excuses for the bullying or blamed themselves, denying or minimizing abuse as a way to survive it.

- All of the targets to varying degrees developed physical health problems.

- Over 60 percent of the targets reported symptoms consistent with Post Traumatic Stress Disorder (PTSD).

- Almost everyone described the experience as one of the worst they have ever encountered.

- Everyone indicated that the experience had a negative impact on their relationship with family members and close friends.

- In some cases, bullying was a factor in a marital breakdown.

- Almost a quarter considered suicide; there were a number of attempted suicides and a number of actual suicides.

- 60 percent described the CEO of their organization as a bully.

- A culture of fear existed in most of the organizations.

- Bullying was condoned in the majority of the organizations.

- Because of the culture of fear very few reported the bullying.

- In a few cases bystanders did become witnesses and defenders.

- Where the bystanders did become witnesses and defenders, most were retaliated against.

- Bystanders became accomplices to the bully in over half of the cases.

- In the few cases where there was an investigation, there was an unsatisfactory outcome for the target.

- Just under half of the organizations had workplace violence/bullying/harassment policies and procedures in place. Most felt the policies, procedures, and programs were meaningless.

- Over 80 percent felt that Human Resources in their organizations was part of the problem.

I want this book to make a difference, and I know it can. In June of 2011, I gave a convocation address where I talked about bullying. The following is an email that I received from a parent of one of the graduates.

> Andrew Faas:
>
> *I am only hoping that this is the Andrew Faas that recently spoke at the graduating class on Saturday. If this is you I would like to tell you that your speech on that day impacted myself and my wife and family in a way that is hard to describe. You see the day before I had to quit my job of just over twenty-five years of service to a management bully who has only been there for just shy of two years. I tried to talk to the higher up management about this but was never taken seriously, they always sided with management. It's hard to say that I had to quit my job as I have never had to leave a job before. Your speech regarding the thought of what goes through people's minds...people going postal is exactly what I have said and that it is harder not to go postal than it is. Also the thought about suicide in your speech impacted me, although I would never think about it but I'm sure many people do. I tried to find you after the ceremony to tell you that you were my hero. I could not believe that this goes on every day and I only hope that it stops. Hearing your speech that day made me feel that I was not alone. Thank you, Andrew, for a speech that will stick with me for years to come. Just a little note also to say that I start a new job where I'm sure that I will be happy on Monday.*
>
> —From a proud parent, graduating class 2011

Prologue

Entrapment

The targets, who are usually solid employees become what the bully wants them to become, poor performers with bad attitudes, thereby giving the bully the ammunition to get rid of them. Bullying is all about power and control. Bullies are masters of deflection, who deceive and manipulate to achieve their end. Both organizations and individuals fall prey, and in doing so usually become entrapped.

Throughout my career I have dealt with many bullying situations, in most cases effectively stopping the bullying. Also in a number of cases I, changed organizational cultures where bullying was tolerated and even encouraged. While I'm proud of this record, I can also recall situations where bullies convinced me into believing that the targets were the culprits.

Reflecting on those situations where I got sucked in (i.e. fell into the *Bully's Trap*) motivated me to help those who are/were targeted and as important, force change in organizational cultures where bullying is tolerated and encouraged.

The Bully's Trap

Vera's story

In July of 2010, Vera was given an option to resign or be fired from her position as a marketing manager for an appliance manufacturer, a position she held for nine years. The reasons given for her termination were poor performance and insubordination. Not wanting to jeopardize her ability to relocate, she agreed to resign and received a modest severance.

Vera's last formal performance review was in February of 2009, where she received an "exceeds expectations" rating. In 2009, Vera received a merit increase which was above average, and incentive payout which recognized that she met all of her individual performance objectives. Over the previous eight years, Vera was rated and viewed as a high performer.

In August of 2009 as part of a restructuring, Vera's reporting relationship changed and Mark, who was also a marketing manager, became the director of the department and Vera's boss. Vera felt that she was more qualified than Mark, but recognized that he had more of a presence, which, in the culture of the organization, counted for more. While Vera was disappointed that she was not promoted, she indicated to Mark that she would support him.

When they were peers, Mark always viewed Vera as a threat. Anytime there was an opportunity to upstage her, he would, and he received credit for work that she had done. Vera's former boss recognized this and would always tell her not to worry about it, that this was just part of Mark's aggressive nature, and that she would get credit for the contributions she made. Over the years, Vera and Mark were given equal exposure to senior executives to review marketing plans and major initiatives. Usually Vera would do most of the prep work and Mark would make the presentation. Vera was okay with this as she was not comfortable with public speaking. During the discussion periods, however, it was apparent that Vera was better prepared than Mark, a classic case of style over substance.

When Mark became the director, he started excluding Vera from the monthly marketing review meetings with senior management. Vera continued to prepare the presentations and the only feedback she got was when Mark could not answer a question, blaming Vera for not having prepped him well enough. Although for the subsequent meetings Vera added a number of notes for Mark to refer to, anticipating the questions he would be asked, Mark continued to have difficulty during the discussion periods. When the CEO suggested publicly that Vera should attend the meetings, Mark became concerned that if Vera attended these meetings, she would show him up and his position would be in jeopardy. Mark's resolution to this was to get rid of Vera.

Mark met with the vice president he reported to and Tim, the head of human resources, and indicated that he was dissatisfied with Vera's work, and he wanted to let her go. The vice president and head of human resources challenged Mark on the basis that Vera had always received a favorable performance review and the previous director thought very highly of her. Mark countered that the previous director covered up Vera's deficiencies, that he (Mark) carried most of the weight and Vera resented the fact that she was not promoted. He also insinuated that Vera and the previous director had more than a professional relationship. The head of human resources suggested to Mark that in order to fire Vera, he had to build a case.

From that point, Mark started to build the case. He kept important information from her, excluded her from meetings she needed to attend, gave her unrealistic targets and timelines and constantly badgered her. All of this started to have an impact on both her performance and attitude. When she challenged Mark on this, he would give her a written reprimand citing insubordination, sending copies to the vice president and Tim. Each time a mistake was made, a target or timeline not reached, Vera would receive a written warning, again with copies to the vice president and Tim. In addition to the written warnings, Vera was subject to verbal abuse, threats, and intimidation.

Knowing Mark the way she did, it crossed Vera's mind that she was being set up. Because Mark could prove that her performance was deteriorating, she started to blame herself for the position she was in. This made her more and more irritable, which caused more confrontations with Mark, which gave Mark more ammunition as he built the case.

Others in the department observed some of what was going on and most had their own challenges with Mark. Vera used to have a good working relationship with them; most would seek her help, which she readily gave. When it became apparent to them that she was targeted, everyone in the department shunned her and she was the subject of a lot of water cooler chats. Mark fed the gossip mill by telling people how badly Vera was handling the situation and that she "did not have her boyfriend there to protect her."

Because she was frustrated with the situation and herself, she often lashed out at others in the department. This put a strain on their relationships and was a factor in no one coming to her defense. Their rationalization was that they felt Vera was not handling the situation well and were upset with her attitude. Mark had some of them go to Tim to complain about Vera. Some only went because they were afraid not to, and others happily complied.

When Vera went to her doctor about some of the physical symptoms she was experiencing, the doctor strongly recommended that she go on disability because of the stress that she was under. Vera was told by Tim that the company would not pay disability benefits as they did not consider stress a disability. Tim told her that she was walking on thin ice and that if she went off on disability, it would be viewed as avoiding disciplinary action for performance and attitude and her absence would be without cause, which would result in her termination. Vera decided not to go on disability.

Vera, not knowing what to do next, complained to Tim that she felt that she was being bullied by Mark and was being set up to be fired. Tim defended Mark's actions and behaviors, indicating that the issues centered around Vera's performance and attitude and unless there was a significant improvement the company would have no choice but to terminate her employment. Tim suggested to Vera that a meeting be held to discuss the matter with Mark. Vera was not comfortable with this but felt she had no choice in the matter.

At the meeting, Tim told Mark that Vera had lodged a complaint about being bullied. Mark told Vera and Tim that he was not bullying, but only doing his job, correcting deficiencies and reacting when he felt that Vera was not being respectful. He went on to say that he was sorry that Vera felt the way she did, that he meant no harm. Tim offered that it was his view that this was more of a personality clash and that Mark's style may be a bit aggressive. Mark agreed with this assessment and promised Vera that he would work on his communication with her, adding, "I understand you are still upset with not getting the promotion, but for this to work you have to get over it."

On returning to the department, Mark followed Vera into her office, closed the door and said, "Now you really have gone too f—ing far! How dare you accuse me of bullying? You're the one who started all of this, you have never been any good and you never will be. Why don't you do everyone a favor and quit?" Vera burst into tears and slapped Mark across the face.

Mark picked up the phone, called Tim, and said, "I want you to fire that bitch right now. She just hit me."

Without getting Vera's side of the story, Tim gave Vera the option to be fired or resign.

The bullying did not stop here.

An advertising agency with whom the company had a long-standing relationship thought highly of Vera and offered to hire her, with the understanding that she would not be assigned any work related to her previous employer. When Mark was informed by the CEO of the agency of their intent, he reacted by saying,

"If you hire her, you will lose this account." Vera was not hired and is still looking for employment. She has been blacklisted, and because it's a small world out there it will make it almost impossible for her to gain comparable employment in her field.

Author's note

As you read this book, reflect back on Vera's Story and those of you who have been targeted, make comparisons on what Vera experienced to that of yours.

Part One

What's Culture Got to Do with It?

"It is not the prisoners who need reformation,
it is the prisons."

—Oscar Wilde 1898—The Ballad of Reading Gaol

What's Culture Got to Do with It?

"...ordinary people, simply doing their jobs, without any particular hostility on their part can become agents in a terrible destructive process. Moreover, even when the destructive effects of their work become patently clear and they are asked to carry out actions incompatible with fundamental standards or morality, relatively few people have the resources needed to resist authority"

—Stanley Milgram "The Perils of Obedience"

B ullies bully because they work in environments that allow, condone, encourage, and even expect it. For the bullying to stop, a cultural transformation is required where bullying is not allowed—period!

Rarely a day goes by when there is not a story in the media about abuse of power, inappropriate behavior, corruption and greed on the part of leadership in every segment of our society, worldwide. Whether it is business, industry, government, education, social services or religion, none are immune.

Where this occurs in organizations, in most cases, there also exists a culture of fear.

Reviewing recent examples of organizations who have gone down, or lost reputational value, the wrongdoing that led to the downfall could have been avoided if people within the organization who were in the know came forward and exposed the situation.

I assert that if there were not a culture of fear in those organizations that created the last financial meltdown, the meltdown could have been avoided.

AIG, Bear Stearns and Lehman Brothers are the good examples of cultures of fear, as well all three had CEOs who were also CBOs (Chief Bullying Officers).

The Rise and Fall of Bear Stearns by Allen Greenberg is great reading for anyone in a leadership role. The book effectively describes how an organization went from having what I describe as a Stable culture to a Dictatorial culture, and the consequences of this shift. He also acknowledges that as Chairman of the Board he had little patience for people complaining about the CEO, mistakenly believing that they were personality or style issues.

Allen Greenberg also notes in the book that had he paid closer attention to the indicators of the cultural shift, he would have been able to write a book titled *The Rise and Continued Rise of Bear Stearns*.

Reports that Ernst and Young, the long-time auditors for Lehman Bothers, were investigated for helping Lehman "cook the books" reveal an example of people who could have come forward early and did not.

The main reason that people do not come forward is a fear of retaliation. Consider what Sharron Watkins, the Enron whistleblower, went through after she exposed the wrongdoing there.

Many organizations have put policies, procedures and whistleblower hot lines in place that provide a vehicle for people to report. The sad reality is people do not trust the mechanism, largely because they do not trust their leaders.

In December of 2010 Sheila Fraser, who was the Auditor General of Canada, issued a 375-page scathing report on the tenure of Canada's first Public Sector Integrity Commissioner, Christine Ouimet. This department is responsible for investigating complaints by public service employees of Government wrongdoing. From August 2007 to July 2009, 228 reports were filed. Of these only seven (yes seven!) were investigated, five were closed with no finding of wrongdoing and two remained under investigation!

Also in her investigation, the Auditor General found that Ms. Ouimet bullied her staff, where she "yelled, swore, marginalized and intimidated" certain PSIC employees and that she engaged in reprisal activities. Turnover of staff during Ms Ouimet's tenure was an astounding 50 percent for each of the two years.

On July 18, 2111 Nick Davis of The Guardian Reporter tells how Sean Hoare (now deceased) became a whistleblower and broke the story that destroyed Rupert Murdock's News of the World and humiliated the media mogul. In explaining why he came forward he said, "I want to right a wrong, lift the lid on it, the whole culture. I know, we all know, that the hacking and other stuff is endemic. Because there is so much intimidation in the newsroom, you have people being fired, breaking down in tears, hitting the bottle."

Research on workplace bullying has always detected serious organizational problems.

> "Crime is a logical extension of the sort of behavior that is often considered perfectly respectable in legitimate business."
>
> —Robert Rice (former Attorney General)
> *The Business of Crime*

My own research illustrated the following problems that are evident in toxic cultures. Specifically:

- Leaders score low on the respectability scale.
- There is a disproportionate focus on the short-term results, at the expense of sustainable long-term performance.

- Leaders do not appreciate the risks to brand and reputational value when bullying is exposed.
- Leaders condone lax ethical standards.
- People are considered expendable.
- There is subjectivity and ambiguity in performance management and advancement.
- Fear is a substitute for motivation.
- There are few checks and balances.
- There is little transparency and disclosures.
- There is negligence at the governance level.
- Turf and power are jealously guarded.
- Power can become addictive. Those that abuse power feed on the fear they create.

What Is Culture?

All too often, leaders view culture as something Human Resource people advocate to make people happy or as only relating to organizational values. This is a narrow view. Culture is all about hardcore business issues. Culture is all encompassing. It is how an organization:

- is governed
- is led
- is aligned to values, beliefs, principles, purpose, vision and initiatives
- is structured
- communicates
- makes decisions
- assigns and aligns work
- operates
- measures performance
- holds accountability
- rewards and recognizes
- hires people
- develops people
- advances people
- handles risk
- handles crisis

Diana Baumrind, a clinical and developmental psychologist in the 1960's, identified three parenting styles which influenced family cultures as being Authoritarian, Permissive, and Authoritative.

Similarly organization cultures can be categorized into three distinct types:

> The Dictatorial
> The Disjointed
> and
> The Stable

I encourage you to examine your workplace under these conceptual lenses. In doing this, it is important to note that these models are not categorical, they are more of a continuum to gain an understanding. You will find that your organization or department fits closer to one type, however the dominant ethos within your workplace culture will be the strongest indicator where your workplace fits on the continuum.

The Dictatorial Culture

"Dictatorship, by whatever means, is founded on
the doctrine that the individual amounts to nothing;
that the state is the only one that counts and that men,
women and children were put on earth solely
for the purpose of serving the state."

—Harry S. Truman

D ictatorial culture, whether in a country or an organization, is all about strictly enforcing control over its citizens or employees. Bullies thrive in a dictatorship and are considered heroes.

In this environment, people (including the bullies) live and work in fear. Some who I have interviewed have described their leaders as benevolent dictators in that they portray themselves as demanding but have the best interests of their employees in mind.

Alaa al Aswany, in *The State of Egypt: A Novelist's Provocative Reflections*, wrote, "The concept of the noble thief or the honest whore, is no more than a meaningless fantasy." The same can be said of a benevolent dictator. A dictator uses whatever means to achieve what he wants, including charm and benevolence. The true character comes out when he is crossed or does not achieve what he wants. On the effectiveness of a dictatorial culture Emila Pardo Bazan put it so well when she wrote, "The dictatorship is like an aria that never becomes an opera."

The characteristics of a dictatorial culture:

• The boss is a tyrant.

• Managers follow the boss's lead.

- Bullying is a means of survival (and advancement).
- It is hierarchical and bureaucratic.
- The boss does not get told what needs to be heard.
- People who "suck up" are favored.
- When things go wrong, employees are blamed and punished.
- Innovation, loyalty, good husbandry and good will are nonexistent.
- There is little to no transparency.
- There is an obsession with secrecy.
- Blind obedience is expected.
- Turf is jealously guarded.

L. Festinger in "A Theory of Cognitive Dissonance" asserts that cultures can alter human behavior. Festinger argues that people will change their "attitudes, beliefs and actions" and or rationalize the changes by "justifying, blaming and denying." Further he notes that "People can be highly impressionable and obedient when provided with a legitimized ideology and social and institutional support, especially when it is done through coercive means by an authority." The Stanford Prison Study and Milgram Experiment illustrate this.

Stanford Prison study

In 1971 Psychology Professor Dr. Philip Zimbardo at Stanford University led a team of researchers to do a study of the psychological effects of becoming a prisoner or guard.

Twenty-four undergraduates were selected to play either a guard or a prisoner. They were randomly selected.

The guards easily adapted to their role using inhuman techniques to degrade and destroy their wards. So brutal were the techniques used that five of the prisoners quit the experiment early and the entire study was stopped (much to the chagrin of the guards) early.

The experimenters said, "approximately one-third of the guards exhibited sadistic tendencies. Most of the guards were upset when the experiment concluded early. The prisoners also internalized their roles and grew increasingly passive and depressive." The results of the experiment conclude that the "situation caused the participants' behaviors, rather than anything inherent in their individual personalities." This study also validates the Milgram experiment which found that because of the situation or culture "...ordinary people without any hostility on their part, can become agents in a terrible destructive process."

The Milgram Experiment

In July of 1961, after the trial of German Nazi war criminal Adolf Eichmann, Stanley Milgram, a Yale University psychologist, conducted a series of experiments to measure "the willingness of the study participants to obey a figure of authority, who instructed them to perform acts that conflicted with their personal conscience."

Milgram summarized the experiment in his 1973 Harper's Magazine article, "The Perils of Obedience," writing:

"The legal and philosophic aspects of obedience are of enormous importance, but they say very little about how most people behave in concrete situations. I set up a simple experiment at Yale University to test how much pain an ordinary citizen would inflict on another person simply because he was ordered to by an experimental scientist. Stark authority was pitted against the subjects' (participants') strongest moral imperatives against hurting others, and, with the subjects' (participants') ears ringing with the screams of the targets, authority won more often than not. The extreme willingness of adults to go to any lengths on the command of an authority constitutes the chief finding of the study and the fact most urgently demanding explanation.

...ordinary people, simply doing their jobs, without any particular hostility on their part, can become agents in a terrible destructive process. Moreover, even when the destructive effects of their work become patently clear and they are asked to carry out actions incompatible with fundamental standards of morality, relatively few people have the resources needed to resist authority."

Bridgegate, the scandal surrounding New Jersey Governor Chris Christie, is more about the culture in Christie's administration than the irresponsible, vindictive and retaliatory actions of his closest aides and allies in the Port Authority in crippling traffic in Fort Lee, New Jersey, for four days in September 2013. Christie has forcefully asserted "I am not a bully" and claims not to have been aware or involved. While there is not yet a smoking gun linking him directly to the incident, Christie does have a reputation of being retaliatory and a bully; therefore, I am doubtful that he was not aware, if not involved. If he was not aware or involved there is clearly a culture in his administration which condones and encourages this type of action. David Gergen, who is senior political analyst for CNN and has served as an advisor to four US Presidents, used Richard Nixon and Watergate as an analogy by indicating that perhaps they did not know or were not directly involved but they created a climate where their staffs did what they would want. Christie like Nixon is a micro manager who wants to be aware of everything, so again it is dubious as to whether he was aware or involved. If his denials are true then one could argue that he has created a culture where his people (both those directly involved and others who were in the know) were afraid to tell him. My bet is that as time goes on other incidents will be exposed.

Case Study—From Canada's National Symbol to Canada's National Shame

The Royal Canadian Mounted Police (RCMP)— An Example of a Dictatorial Culture

The image of a police officer on a horse in a scarlet coat and wide-brimmed hat is Canada's most recognized symbol. Established in 1864, with headquarters in Saskatchewan, the Mounties evolved into a hugely complex police force with close to 30,000 employees.

Once an international icon of solid Canadian Values, the RCMP has found itself mired in a litany of organizational, legal and political controversies. In July 2010 the Canadian Broadcasting Service in a documentary called *Mounties Under Fire* described them as having a "broken culture."

The stated Core Values of the RCMP are:

"Recognizing the dedication of all employees, we will create and maintain an environment of individual safety, well-being and development. We are guided by:

- Integrity
- Honesty
- Professionalism
- Compassion
- Respect
- Accountability"

Based on a number of reports and surveys done, it appears that these values are nothing but propaganda, and that they are guided by the exact opposite of these.

When I look at the history and instances from 1978 to now, the RCMP stands out as an organization with serious organizational problems that has most of the characteristics of a Dictatorial culture. What really stands out most are the denials, cover- ups and efforts to "keep it in the family."

The RCMP is structured on a paramilitary model which operates on a command and control hierarchy. Until 2006 they were allowed to operate with a high degree of autonomy and independence. The Government finally recognized that the wrong doings (which were getting a fair bit of media attention) could no longer be overlooked. A committee to investigate the allegations was established. Commissioner Giuliano Zaccerdelli appeared before the committee and admitted he made mistakes and earlier gave the committee inaccurate testimony. He submitted his resignation to the Prime Minister the next day.

The departure of Zaccerdelli was not sufficient to change the culture. The RCMP is an insular organization, steeped in antiquated traditions which are counterproductive for a modern police force (or any other organization). The culture of fear is maintained to cover up problems, preserve traditions, preserve the right of rank and resist change.

An internal RCMP report in 2010, entitled "RCMP Values, Driven Leadership" suggests that the workplace culture is badly in need of repair across the country and that bad management by some supervisors is "creating a toxic workplace, high levels of stress, and a culture of fear."

This report contains details about the use of sick leave. At the time of the report 336 employees in British Columbia alone were on long-term disability with some having been on leave for up to seven years, and that health professionals estimate that 75 percent of those on sick leave are there for post traumatic stress disorder or "because of conflicts with supervisors and others within the organization."

In his book *Inside the Secret World of Ottawa and the RCMP,* Paul Palango describes the cult mentality that exists. A highly regarded former officer describes the culture this way, "The RCMP resists any criticism, and it does not respect the public, bureaucrats, or politicians. If one of the brass gets involved in a controversy, there is no will within the force to assess the person's culpability. The saying is, Respect the rank, not the story." The book also details where charges of abuse, assault, harassment and deceit were routinely made to disappear.

In 2009 the RCMP conducted a national survey to gauge morale, a process it undertakes every two years. The survey found that one in four employees in British Columbia had been "verbally harassed or tormented" within the past year. "Organizational culture" received the worst score of all, fifty-five questions and only 17 percent felt that the survey would make any difference. The survey also revealed that nearly 60 percent of RCMP employees have considered quitting their job in the past six months. Frustration and lack of recognition are the most common reasons, according to the survey.

In 2003 a scandal surrounded the administration of the force's pension and insurance plans, where there were allegations of fraud and abuse during the outsourcing of the plans. An independent investigator was appointed by the Federal Government. While the scandal was significant enough in and unto itself to taint the force, the review highlighted a fundamental flaw in the culture; rather than encouraging disclosure of wrongdoing, senior management retaliated against employees who brought the wrongdoings forward. The investigator's report, titled "Restoring the Honour of the RCMP: December 2007," concluded "RCMP senior management allowed an unethical culture to develop, which discouraged the disclosing of wrong doing and did not hold individuals to account for unethical behavior." This committee commended the people who were viewed as whistleblowers by senior management "as exemplifying the stated values of the RCMP, and those who subjected these people to reprisals expressed the exact opposite."

Professor Linda Duxbury of Carlton University in Ottawa conducted an extensive survey of RCMP members, which found extreme frustration with managers. "What they were frustrated with was the top down style of management, non supportive managers who don't trust or respect their members, manager's inability to communicate effectively with staff, politically driven agendas, managers who are perceived to be careerists who are governed by their personal agendas and managers who do not walk the talk."

In the September 2007 issue of Mcleans Canada, Sara Scott wrote an article called "Is this the end of the Toxic Boss? Judges are sending corporate bullies a message; treat your employees with respect." In the article she highlights the RCMP, citing the case of Officer Nancy Sulz, a $50,000 per year police officer with eight years experience who won nearly one million dollars from the RCMP for being bullied by a senior officer.

The crisis within the RCMP hit a peak in July of 2010 when the Commissioner, William Elliot, was accused of being a bully by ten deputy and assistant Commissioners who took their complaints directly to the Prime Minister's office. This was an unprecedented airing of dirty laundry for a notoriously insular organization.

Initially the Government decided to support Commissioner Elliot (the first civilian and first external Commissioner) because they recognized that he was trying to change the toxic culture, and agreed with Elliot's assertion that those who were against the changes were trying to force him out (a classic tactical move by bullies). In the summer of 2011 the bullies won when Elliott decided to resign.

In November of 2011 Bob Paulson, a lifelong Mountie who promised to conduct a review of outstanding complaints of harassment, was appointed as the new Commissioner. "Culture" was cited as the sixth issue in an article by Laura Payton and Alison Crawford called "7 Issues Facing the RCMP Commissioner" for the CBC News on October 27th, 2011. "Mounties knew about it for years but it was only through the publication of Brown's report that the general public learned about the RCMP's so called penalty box culture where people who questioned authority were bullied, seconded to other government departments or sent on interminable French training."

Paulson is now being challenged as a man of words only because of his failure to deliver on his commitment to positively change the culture where trust in the institution is regained. His dismissive attitude on harassment claims reviewed by a senate committee in 2013 and efforts by some to unionize as only representing disgruntled employees is seriously jeopardizing his position to make the changes he has promised.

In 2012 Staff Sergeant Granvelle, who was the harassment, human rights and alternative dispute resolution coordinator for the Atlantic region, herself had to file a rights complaint because she was threatened with dismissal for filing complaints against her supervisor. In October of 2013 Janet Merlo, a 20 year veteran RCMP Officer, wrote a book called *No One To Tell, Breaking My Silence on Life in the RCMP* in which she asserts that not much has changed since Paulson's appointment.

In July of 2014 an officer who suffered from Post Traumatic Stress Disorder, and was forced to retire, committed suicide. Family members claim that the force does not do enough to address the stigma of mental illness and a recent audit found that close to forty percent of RCMP employees who are on long term disability, cite mental health problems.

The Disjointed Culture

The disjointed culture can best be described as a loose federation. It is a culture that tries to accommodate everyone. Like a dictatorial culture it is hierarchical and bureaucratic, and process is a substitute for purpose. Usually departments and regional locations operate in silos. There are few checks and balances and bullies can and do operate freely. Here, as in the dictatorial culture bullies are usually considered high performers and heroes. Those who are bullied and the bystanders do not trust the systems in place to report abuse for fear of retaliation.

Characteristics of a Disjointed Culture:

- There is a lack of structure and discipline.
- Rules are not consistently applied.
- Events are reactionary.
- Rituals are substitutes for core values.
- There is a cover-up mentality.
- There is a lack of alignment to purpose, values, operating principles, vision and initiatives (usually because there are none or there are too many).
- There is ambiguity and subjectivity in performance management (metrics, rewards, recognition and advancement).
- Cronyism and nepotism are evident.

- It is highly emotional and reactionary.

- Best practice, state of the art employment policies are evident but in practice nonexistent.

- Leaders live with false delusions.

- People are allowed to discredit others.

- Where there are multiple locations, it is a loose federation of companies operating in silos.

- Turf is jealously guarded.

- There is little to no transparency.

The Catholic Church— An Example of a Disjointed Culture

John Thavis in his book *The Vatican Diaries* provides a behind-the-scenes look at the power, personalities, and politics at the heart of the Catholic Church. This book was published just before the resignation of Pope Benedict.

The Vatican that Pope Francis inherited has a culture that is disjointed and dysfunctional.

It is encouraging to witness the new Pope's recognition that the Catholic Church needs to restore its reputation of being respected defenders of human rights, peace, and social justice. To do this he must initiate a cultural transformation. The Pope's comments on gay priests, the senior appointments he has made, and his resolve to change the Vatican Bank are great indicators of changes that are necessary.

Although the initial words and actions are positive, it is yet to be seen whether Pope Francis can break the stronghold of the hierarchy and the various autonomous orders. Being the first Pope from the Jesuit Order is a significant indicator as the Jesuit's more closely resembles that of what I define as a stable culture—plus they have great resolve and discipline.

On December 22, 2014 Pope Francis used his annual Christmas Greeting to outline plans to fix the culture within the church. Holding back no punches he gave a scathing criticism of the culture and denounced those who "have sought power at the expense of others and those who have acted rigid, tough and arrogant."

The Stable Culture

Values and beliefs are at the core of stable cultures. There is the recognition that people are the key component to the success of the organization. The stable culture sets high but reasonable expectations, holds people accountable for performance, behaviors and actions, provides what is necessary for people to excel, fairness and equity rank high as values and team trumps any individual recognition.

Characteristics of a Stable Culture:

- There is a governance model in place that monitors beyond the financials.

- There is a common and well understood vision and purpose.

- Values and operating principles are bed rocked as a foundation.

- Rules (a code of conduct and terms of engagement) are simply stated and consistently applied.

- There is an effective and inclusive strategic planning process that proportionately focuses more on sustainable, long-term performance and emphasises agility to respond to ever-changing market conditions.

- All internal stakeholders are aligned to the vision, values, operating principles and the plan.

- Roles, responsibilities and accountability are clearly defined.

- Vendor and Government relations are positive and fair.

- A four-dimensional, balanced score card measurement system is in place (customer, employee, financial and execution).

- The four R's are rigorously followed (doing the RIGHT things, the RIGHT way, by the RIGHT people at the RIGHT time).

- Competency and co-operation are modeled and encouraged.

- Team is valued over individual.

- People are taught to think.

- People are motivated to be all they can be.

- People are measured more by the quality of their contributions than the quantity of output and time spent.

- There is a clear value exchange model in place (clear expectations of employees are set against what employees should expect from the organization to deliver on what the organization expects of them).

- Bosses and subordinates have regular, equal conversations, during which the boss asks things like "What do you need from me to deliver on what we have to achieve?"

- Leaders hear what they need to know.

- There is no fear of retaliation, and people are comfortable in bringing forward ideas, issues and opportunities.

- Courage is highly valued.

- Mistakes are considered learning opportunities.

- There is a high level of transparency.

Case Study—On Becoming a Stable Culture—Shoppers Drug Mart (circa 1998-2008)

It is not unusual to have subcultures within an organization, i.e.: where the overall culture is dictatorial or disjointed and some departments or locations have stable cultures, or conversely where the corporate culture is stable and some of the departments or locations have dictatorial or disjointed ones.

Having spent the bulk of my career in retail (twenty-three years with Loblaw Companies Ltd—Canada's largest food retailer—and ten years with Shoppers Drug Mart), overseeing in excess of one thousand locations, I have witnessed firsthand the dynamics of sub-cultures and the resulting impact on performance. At Shoppers Drug Mart, Canada's largest drug store chain, where I was a management partner for ten years, we built a positive high performance culture—what I refer to as a "Stable Culture."

In 1999 when we carried out a management-led buyout (with KKR, Bain Capital, Charles Bank, DLJ and Ontario Teachers Pension Plan), we assessed that while overall performance was respectable, it was not performing to its full potential—the market was growing at a faster rate than we were, there where inconsistencies across the chain in staffing levels, store conditions, pricing, hours of operation, in stock positions, adherence to national programs—in essence the only consistency was inconsistency.

Unfortunately almost all of the senior management team had to be replaced—they had the technical capabilities, but as they fundamentally disagreed with the massive change that was required, we recognized early on that the prerequisite step was to have a team in place that bought into the plan. Most of the existing team were not on side as they felt their turf and base of power was at risk.

Glenn Murphy, someone I worked with at Loblaw's, was hired as Chair and CEO.

The new team we selected, with a few exceptions, were promoted from within. We chose well, as they became one of the most aligned, driven, and cohesive teams I have had the pleasure of working with.

Immediately following the buyout, we embarked on a program to totally transform the organization. The first step was conducting a cultural assessment of the corporate and regional offices followed by an assessment of all store locations.

Poor and marginal performing stores were benchmarked against comparable high performers. What we found was most of the high performing stores had the characteristics of a Stable culture and most of the poor and marginal performers had the characteristics of Dictatorial or Disjointed cultures. Bullying was evident in many of the corporate departments, the regional offices, and in the store locations which had the characteristics of Dictatorial and Disjointed cultures.

In tangible terms, we found the high performance stores had sustainable financial results, lower employment costs both in absolute dollars and as a percent of sales, higher customer satisfaction scores, lower staff attrition, higher sales per square foot, higher sales per transaction, higher in stock positions and higher inventory turns, and a higher sell through of seasonal items. We also heard directly from our customers, because of the inconsistencies in our offerings and their shopping experiences we were "over promising and under delivering."

To realize full potential we needed to significantly increase store count and operating hours, including additional 24-hour locations, extending hours and being open on Sundays and holidays.

A huge challenge was our reliance on pharmacists. Under legislation, drug stores cannot open, even for an hour, without a pharmacist on site. When we hired new pharmacists, it was like pouring water into a bucket with a big hole in the bottom. The attrition rate was over 30 percent and the vacancy run rate was just over 20 percent. To add to the dilemma, at the time, there was a worldwide shortage of pharmacists.

This alone was sufficient reason to go through a cultural transformation—ensuring all locations had a stable one. To reach our growth objectives we needed to become an "Employer of Choice."

The transformation was complete within a year. It was hard work and we initially met with significant resistance at all levels. We cut through a lot of it by distinguishing what people disliked about the proposed changes, against what they disagreed with because they felt it was fundamentally wrong, making the point that "because you don't like or agree with something does not mean it is wrong—it may be different than what you would like or do, but is not necessarily wrong." Making this distinction and only debating what they fundamentally disagreed with vs. what they did not like allowed us to move quickly. Many organizational transformations are derailed because of resistors who feel the changes will erode their autonomy or power.

Post our cultural transformation the variances in the performance indicators of the entire network of stores was dramatically reduced and the overall performance of the organization dramatically improved—specifically within five years the number of stores doubled, our EPS went from less than $1 to $2.64, the enterprise value went from $5 per share to $58, we became the "employer of choice" and the attrition and vacancy rate for pharmacists went to a low single digit.

Altering the Attitudes of Organizational Leaders

The attitudes that organizational leaders have on bullying in the workplace is the single biggest determiner as to whether an organization is free and safe from bullying.

If leadership does not understand what constitutes bullying and are unaware of the consequences to the individual, organization and the community, bullying will be condoned and even encouraged.

If leadership believes that bullying is an effective tactic to achieve results, bullying will certainly be condoned and encouraged.

If the CEO is also the CBO (Chief Bullying Officer) bullying will not only be condoned and encouraged; managers throughout the organization will be expected to bully.

To understand the mindset of organizational leaders on bullying, 138 leaders were interviewed—seventy-two CEOs, twenty-six Executive Directors, and forty Board Chairs across Canada and The United States. Of the 138, thirty-three were women.

These leaders represent a cross section of organizations, private and public, government, health care, manufacturing, financial services, retail, technology, transportation and resources. All but twenty-one of the organizations had multi locations and the number of employees ranged from a low of just under four hundred to a high of 64,000. Employees in sixteen of the organizations were represented by a union or an association.

The methodology used was a structured but open-ended face-to-face discussion with each to gain qualitative insights. I do not claim this to be a scientific study; however, the findings and observations validate and are consistent with the findings and observations on the interviews conducted with over 300 people who either have been bullied or have someone close to them who has been bullied.

With most of the leaders interviewed there was a debate on what constituted bullying. Most would not accept the definition and viewed what I described as the ways and means of bullying as more of an aggressive management style. All did acknowledge however that sexual and racial harassment was wrong and should be considered bullying. These debates at the front end of the discussion helped put the overall discussions in context. While most felt my definition was too extreme, all but a few accepted it for the purpose of the discussion.

As the purpose was to gain an understanding on their attitudes and level of awareness, the interviews conducted avoided debating the rightness or wrongness of bullying.

The Findings:

1. The overall level of awareness and understanding of what constitutes bullying (and what does not) is low. Most do not view bullying as workplace violence.

2. Although most want their organizations to be viewed as employers of choice and rate brand and reputation value as a high priority, few view bullying as a business risk in their organization.

3. The overall level of awareness and understanding of the impact that bullying has on the individual, organization and community is low.

4. When given our definition of bullying and the ways and means of bullying, all but seventeen indicated that they at some point in their careers have been targeted. Ironically many described their experiences and those of others they are close to with great indignation.

5. 73 percent of the CEOs indicated that they could argue they were being bullied by their Board of Directors because of the pressure for short-term results.

6. All but three of the Executive Directors of the not for profit organizations indicated that they spend a disproportionate amount of their time dealing with unreasonably difficult Board members.

7. 67 percent acknowledged that they use bullying as a tactic to get things done, improve productivity and or get better deals.

8. 69 percent believe that those who are targeted have performance or attitudinal issues, therefore, with the exception of sexual or racial bullying, it is warranted.

9. 71 percent condone bullying because they believe that fear is a better motivator than what they refer to as "that human resources stuff."

10. The notion that bullying causes targets to reduce their level of engagement, commitment and performance was widely rejected.

11. 52 percent of the leaders who operate where there is workplace violence and/or anti-bullying legislation were aware of the legislation. Those who were aware felt that their organizations were compliant; and only 7 percent could describe what compliant meant.

12. 86 percent indicated that they would not educate their employees on bullying because of a concern that employees

would use bullying as a sword or a shield when they are subjected to disciplinary action.

13. While 62 percent indicated that they had stated values and operating principles only 14 percent of the sixty-two could recite what they were.

14. Only 27 percent could give adequate answers to cultural indicators [staff turnover (resignation rate), reasons people cite for leaving (absentee rate), number of people on stress leave, participation rate of engagement surveys, participation rate of people using EAP, history of human rights complaints].

15. Of the forty Board Chairs interviewed, six indicated their boards reviewed some of the cultural indicators.

16. 54 percent measure beyond the financials and 44 percent of this group uses a balanced scorecard methodology.

17. Of the thirty-four who had to deal with instances of bullying only four found the alleged bully to be at fault.

18. 69 percent considered staff turnover as a positive as it "gets rid of dead weight" and "allows for new blood."

19. 51 percent acknowledged that employees in their organizations may be afraid to report wrongdoings.

20. 86 percent felt that whistleblowers should be required to absolutely prove the allegation.

21. 52 percent consider whistleblowers treasonous.

22. 63 percent recognized that they may not be hearing what they need to hear.

23. 76 percent indicated that they often accept one-sided representations when there is a conflict or disagreement.

24. 71 percent feel it is healthy to create a certain amount of conflict because "it makes people competitive."

25. 32 percent manage by "walking around."

26. 24 percent used the latest economic downturn to "clean house." Most of this group challenged their managers to force people out rather than lay them off.

Based on the work I have done in the area and my analysis of interviews conducted, it is my assessment that:

- Bullying is not considered to be an issue.

- More than half of the organizational leaders are bullies.

- Because of the pressure to deliver on short-term results most organizational leaders condone and encourage bullying to force productivity and force people out.

- The attitudes that organizational leaders have on bullying begets bullies throughout organizations. Bullies become the heroes and the bullied become not only the targets but also the villains (bullied bullies).

- As long as results are achieved, boards of directors are not interested in whether or not bullying goes on. Note point 14 above where only 27 percent of organizational leaders could give adequate answers to cultural indicators.

- Organizational leaders view fear as a more effective motivator than performance management systems.

- Workplace violence and anti-bullying legislation is viewed as an unnecessary aggravation that is relegated to either legal or human resources to fulfill the bare minimum.

- Short of a "going postal" situation, bullying will not be considered an issue with most organizational leaders.

- There is a fear that by raising the level of awareness on bullying, there will be abuse by employees, accusing managers of bullying when they try to correct deficiencies, and managers will become afraid to manage.

⤜

The scandal at Rutgers University illustrates the attitudes of organizational leadership on bullying.

In the fall of 2012 a video exposed Mike Rice, The Scarlet Kings men's basketball coach, verbally and physically abusing players. The President, Robert L. Barchi, was made aware of the video in November of 2012, but claims he did not view it. An ethics committee made up of board members and trustees did view it at a December 14th meeting and were satisfied that the three-game suspension Rice received was adequate.

Barchi, in defending his role, placed blame on the athletic director, Tim Pernette, and other officials, saying they decided to follow a process involving university lawyers, human resource professionals, and outside counsel. This is based on a report that was commissioned that recommended that Rice be suspended and sent to an anger management course.

The fifty-page report, conducted by an outside lawyer, made clear that Rice's outbursts "were not isolated" and that "he had a fierce temper, used homophobic and misogynistic slurs, kicked his players and threw basketballs at them." The report went on to describe him as "passionate, energetic and demanding" and claim that his behaviors constituted "permissible training" and he "caused them to play better during the team's basketball games."

After the video exploded in the media, Barchi had Rice fired. One can only assume the firing was in reaction to the disastrous publicity—not Rice's behavior!

I assert if this case does not prompt leaders to view workplace bullying differently, nothing will.

⤜

There has been much debate on the Miami Dolphins harassment situation. In October of 2013, Jonathan Martin walked away from a multimillion dollar contract with the Miami Dolphins alleging harassment by his teammates, coach, and in particular, the ring leader, Richie Incognito. Incognito, who has a record of abusive behavior, claimed he was asked by the coaching team to "toughen him (Martin) up."

People I have spoken to about this have generally had the attitude that what happened to Martin was appropriate as football is a tough game and if players can't take the heat they should get out. My counter to this argument is using boot camps in the military as an analogy. There is no question that it would be irresponsible not to test and train soldiers for physical and emotional endurance, and the intent of boot camps is to strengthen the individual before they are sent into harm's way.

My analysis of what happened to Martin is that Incognito's intention and the tactics he used were to destroy rather than strengthen.

In conditioning people to work in dangerous or tough environments the use of racial and homophobic slurs, threats, innuendoes and demanding questionable actions effectively weaken the target to the point they want out which, in my view is what happened to Martin in February 2014. The National Football League's independent investigators found that this is a cultural issue within the Miami Dolphins largely due to the attitude of the coaching and management team.

Bullying and Board Governance

"Good governance does not just prevent misdeeds
but actually improves the corporation."

—Ram Charan

How accountable are boards of directors for bullying that occurs in organizations they govern? As governance models continue to evolve, there is no clear answer. A better question is should boards be held accountable when bullying occurs and should they be responsible for ensuring that people in the organization are free and safe from bullying? I assert they should be. Bullying in the workplace exposes an organization to risk. As boards are responsible for protecting and growing enterprise value for the shareholder, anything that puts at risk the brand, and reputation value, puts at risk the enterprise value. Bullying puts an organization at great risk.

The scandalous frauds and abuses at Enron, WorldCom, Tyco and all too many others revealed gaping holes in the checks and balances that were intended to keep corporations honest and protect stakeholders, which resulted in the massive bankruptcies, cheated investors out of billions, caused massive layoffs and destroyed whole communities. Poor corporate governance has ruined companies; it destroyed a global accounting firm and threatened economies and governments. This has resulted in calls for board reform. For years directors have viewed that they are only responsible to the shareholder and have not factored in their owing a duty to other stakeholders including employees, customers, suppliers and any parties whose interests may be impacted by the organizations actions. For many that includes communities affected by local employment, environmental hazards or the exploitation of natural resources.

The primary role of a board is strategy formulation and policymaking; their accountability, however, is reduced when they do not consider that they are accountable for how the strategy and policies get implemented. This and the failures of oversight mechanisms expose directors to considerable litigation risk as they are de facto the first and last defence for fiduciary responsibility. Whether it is boards being let down by management, or they are asleep at the switchboards, they must step-up and major reforms are essential.

In *Money for Nothing*, John Gillespie and David Zeiwing describe the failure of corporate boards and exposes the flaws of a dysfunctional system. While the focus of the book is on shareholder rights, the authors recognize the other stakeholders by advocating "In modern economic thinking boards should also monitor the interests of employees, customers, suppliers, creditors and the communities and the environment in which a firm operates, because these interests can be critical to increasing the long term value of the shareholders investment."

The suicide of Pierre Wauthier CFO of Zurich Insurance in August of 2013 has highlighted the risk of a toxic culture as investor confidence has been shaken by the suicide and suggestions that Wauther was subject to excessive pressure. After the suicide the company announced that the board was launching a cultural review. According to board governance guru Ram Charan in his books, *Owning Up* and *Boards That Deliver*, good governance does not just prevent misdeeds but actually improves the corporation.

Governance now means leadership, and gone are the days when board members would ceremoniously sit on boards, gathering prestige, and ensuring the company was in compliance with the rules and regulations of the industry. In pointing to the aim of progressive boards, Charan quotes Andy Grove, founder, former CEO and Chair of Intel: "[A progressive board aims] to ensure that the success of a company is longer lasting than any CEO's reign, than any market opportunity, than any product cycle."

In analyzing organizations that have had a reversal of fortune, and those who have gone down, a major factor was the profile of the CEO. The CEOs were also CBOs. Many have argued that there was no way to see the subprime mortgage crisis coming. We now know there were those who did, who blew the whistle, but were not heard because of CBOs who would not allow voices of dissent to be heard. CBOs see the organization as an extension of their own egos. This usually results in a hostile and toxic culture that costs companies dearly in lost productivity and intellectual capital, and has caused the downfall of many organizations. The question that must be asked here is: Were where the directors?

Lehman Brothers and AIG are two good examples of companies who could have survived and prospered if they had the benefit of better governance. On a much larger scale, the global financial meltdown could have been avoided had there been better governance.

Lehman Brothers was a storied institution that survived two World Wars, the Great Depression, and practically every other calamity in its 158-year history, but was brought down in the largest bankruptcy by the their CEO Richard Fuld, also known as "the Gorilla" because of his bullying. Many of his critics have blamed his bullying as the direct cause of Lehman's downfall. Fuld bullied everyone around him and created a culture of fear and intimidation to the extent that even the Lehman directors were afraid of him. The longest tenured CEO on Wall Street, Fuld kept his job as the subprime mortgage crisis took hold, while CEOs of the other institutions were forced to resign. The Lehman board remained reluctant to challenge Fuld as the firms share price spiralled lower and lower.

In his book, *A Colossal Failure of Common Sense,* insider Lawrence G. McDonald had this to say: "King Richard had even turned Lehman's board of directors into a kind of largely irrelevant lower chamber. This was yet another group to rubber-stamp his decisions and collect generous fees. It was not for supplying well-meant and lucid wisdom in the current wild market-place, but for agreeing with the monarch, accepting his all-knowing take on the bank's investments. Above all, the board was not to rock the royal barge as it made its steady way down the stream."

One bad boss may be responsible for bringing AIG, the U.S. Economy, and the global financial system to their knees. Joe Cassano: The Man Who Crashed the World, as he was labeled by Michael Lewis in the August 2009 feature in *Vanity Fair,* or "Patient Zero of the Global Economic Meltdown" as nicknamed by Matt Tiabbi in Rolling Stone magazine, Cassano may be the world's poster boy CBO.

Cassano did become widely known as a bully across AIG, where the view of the boss was consistent, "a guy with a crude feel for financial risk, but a real talent for bullying people who doubted him." "AIG became a dictatorship" says one London trader. "Joe would bully people around. He'd humiliate them..." As in the case of Lehman Brothers, where was the board in all of this? Afraid and negligent.

Human Resources—Part of the Problem or Part of the Solution?

When I go into organizations to do an assessment, it is usually when the organization is in serious trouble or after a major incident. The first thing I attempt to determine is the role that human resources plays in influencing culture.

In many organizations and the many cases that I have dealt with, I have found that well over 70 percent of the time human resources is part of the problem versus part of the solution.

In most cases human resource people view bullying as a personality clash or a management style issue and apply conflict resolution techniques to resolve the problem. Usually this makes the situation worse for the target and the bully feels further empowered because they have successfully deflected their predatory behaviors, manipulating human resources to become their ally.

Organizational cultures dictate the role that human resources plays in preventing and stopping bullying.

In Disjointed cultures, human resources are called in after the fact and told to make the problem go away. Here the head of human resources is not a key player and lacks authority to hold bullies accountable. Where there is legislation, policies and procedures are put into place but not into practice. Targets and bystanders do not go to human resources because they know that human resources have no power and/or courage to properly intervene. Heads of human resources in these cultures are usually not equipped to deal with bullying. People working in human resources in these cultures know what bullying is because they are bullied and are cowered into thinking that this goes with the territory.

In Dictatorial cultures, human resources are also called in after the fact and told to make the problem go away. Here the head of human resources could be a key player and if so, is part of the problem. Bullies in these cultures are considered heroes, because they are viewed as high performers and have more credibility than their targets. Bullies know this and manipulate human resources to become their allies. Where there is legislation, policies and procedures are put into place but not into practice, compliance is for legal and security reasons versus prevention. Targets and bystanders do not go to human resources because they do not trust the leadership and by extension, people in human resources. In many cases heads of human resources have the technical and academic credentials to be the best and the brightest in the profession but lack the influence and or courage to prevent and stop bullying from occurring. As in Disjointed cultures, human resource people working in these cultures know what bullying is, because they are bullied, and because of the environment in which they work, they tend to become a bully who is targeted by another bully.

In Stable cultures, human resources are mandated to make employees free and safe from bullying. Here the head of human resources is a key player and has the authority not only to hold bullies accountable but more importantly prevent bullying from occurring. Legislation does not drive putting policies and procedures in place. They have been in place and are firmly entrenched and integrated in the way they conduct all of their affairs. Where there are incidents, human resources conduct a swift but comprehensive investigation and resolve the situation. Targets and bystanders go to human resources because they trust both the system and the individual, and they are viewed as being neutral. Heads of human resources in these cultures are the best and the brightest of their profession because they apply their technical and academic background and experience and view their role as custodians of a positive culture. Human resource people working in these cultures know what bullying is because they have studied the topic.

While the CEO should own and drive the culture of an organization, the head of human resources should be responsible and accountable for the integrity of the cultural health of the organization in the same way the CFO is responsible and accountable for the integrity of the financial systems and reporting.

The head of human resources is in the best position, regardless of the culture, to stop bullying from occurring. This should not be a matter of choice; it is a requirement of the job. If the head of human resources is not equipped or does not have the courage to make it stop, they are in the wrong position and as such, part of the problem.

The following outlines what human resources should do to ensure that the work environment is safe and free from bullying.

1. Conduct a comprehensive annual risk assessment.

2. Report findings and a plan of action to senior management and the board of directors for their endorsement and approval.

3. Develop and institutionalize policies, procedures and programs that address the issue of workplace violence.

4. Include workplace violence in the code of conduct.

5. As part of the hiring of and promotion to a management position process, have a psychological assessment be a condition of acceptance. No exemptions.

6. Develop a "Terms of Engagement" agreement for all senior staff to sign.

7. Ensure that the performance management systems are clear, fair, reasonable, and not ambiguous or subjective, thereby not giving a bully the opportunity to entrap a target.

8. Regularly train managers and supervisors on:

   - Performance Management

   - The policies, procedures and programs

   - Identification of risk behaviors

   - How to recognize, respond, report and prevent bullying

9. Conduct an annual awareness program for all employees outlining their rights and responsibilities on workplace violence.

10. Develop an incident investigation protocol that is swift, fair, objective, comprehensive, and minimizes the risk of the target becoming the villain.

11. In the event the CEO is also the CBO (Chief Bullying Officer), coach and guide him/her on changing their attitudes and behaviors. If they are not successful, they must report this to the Chair of the board of directors for their intervention.

Heads of human resources should view becoming part of the solution as a real opportunity to gain influence and relevance. Key to becoming part of the solution is to have credibility as an honest broker that acts in the best interest of all concerned.

The Red Flags

If bullying is occurring there are always indicators that it is happening. If people in human resources do not monitor these indicators they are part of the problem.

The majority of instances of bullying are not reported by either the target or the bystanders. Just because there are no reports or complaints of bullying does not mean it is not going on. Usually bullying situations are talked about amongst employees and bullies build a reputation. If bullies are not confronted they are in essence allowed to run loose.

Other than employees talking amongst themselves, there are a number of indicators that can identify and expose bullying and the bullies. To be part of the solution people in human resources need to follow up on any and every indicator. Where there is a bully running loose, there is almost always a number of telltale signs, and by tying what may appear to be seemingly unrelated comments, events and situations together, it usually tells a story.

The following outlines the telltale signs that a bully or a number of bullies are running loose:

- The "noise level" or comments that people are making, directly and indirectly. If there is a bully running loose, people will talk about it. People in human resources need to have people in the organization keeping them in the loop when they hear people talking about it. If the other indicators of bullying are there and the people in human resources are not hearing the "noise level" they are out of the loop.

- Anonymous letters from people who are aware of a situation, but are afraid to bring it forward.

- Calls to a whistleblower hot line. If there are no or few calls to the hot line, this is an indicator that there may be a fear factor in reporting wrongdoing.

- Comments made by employees on the social media e.g. blogs. Don't try to stop the blogs or identify employees who post—stop the reasons employees feel it necessary to post.

- High turnover is an indicator that something is amiss. This, connected with other indicators, could expose bullying.

- Exit interviews. When people leave they should be asked whether bullying was a factor in their departure. People may not be direct in their comments, not wanting to burn bridges, but will usually give comments like, "He could be difficult to work with, or demanding, but we just learned to live with it." When comments like these are made, the interviewer should probe and make the person comfortable in giving specifics.

- Increase in the absentee rate.

- Increase in the number of people on stress leave.

- Difficulty in getting people to transfer into a particular department or division.

- Engagement survey data comparison by department.

- Written comments that are made in engagement surveys. A lack of, or few written comments are an indicator that there could be a fear factor in expressing viewpoints or concerns.

- Comments made by vendors, recruiters and other service providers. While these people are external to the organization, they are often bystanders and may hear and see more of what is going on in an organization than what the organizational leaders and human resource people hear and see. These people could also be a bully's target.

- In organizations that have medical departments, regular and ongoing dialogue on levels of stress within the organization.

- Increase in calls made to the EAP (employee assistance program). The providers of these programs should be required to make human resources aware of bullying situations, with the assurance that the target's confidentiality is protected.

- Inconsistencies in representations made by a manager to discipline or terminate a subordinate. (A review of the subordinate's performance history compared to what the manager is representing.)

- Managers who take all the credit when things go well and blame others when things go wrong.

- Individuals who constantly have disputes with others and are unwilling to compromise on their positions.

- Previous accusations or incidences of bullying.

On becoming aware of a situation or the probability of bullying occurring, the onus should be on human resources to check into it immediately.

The first step is to review all indicators that are available which would add credence or discount the allegation or the probability of bullying. This is where it is important to tie the seemingly unrelated comments, events and situations together. As much of this information should be readily available, it should not take an inordinate amount of time to pull together. Depending on the situation, it may be necessary to conduct interviews with people who are close to the situation.

Armed with this information, the human resource person should meet with the suspected bully's immediate supervisor to review the situation and determine who should have a meeting with the suspected bully.

The purpose of the meeting is to outline to the person that bullying is suspected, along with the reasons for suspecting. If there is not a specific complaint and there is no direct evidence, the person should not be accused of being a bully. However, in the discussion it is appropriate to indicate that there are indicators that bullying is occurring and the organization is obliged to investigate and take the necessary steps to make sure that bullying is not occurring.

It is also appropriate to challenge the person on the reasons the indicators are there, for example asking why turnover is high. The ideal outcome is to have the person acknowledge that there is validity to the concerns being raised and agreeing to change the behavior. If this happens the person should be asked what the organization can do to help change the behavior, for example help with anger management. At the end of the meeting it must be pointed out that the expectation will be for the indicators to change, for example lower turnover and a much lower "noise level." In situations where the person denies being a bully and rationalizes the indicators, then a more comprehensive investigation should be conducted. The person who is suspected of being a bully should be made aware of this and that people who are close to the investigation will be interviewed. It should also be made very clear that any intimidation or retaliation against people being interviewed will result in severe disciplinary action, up to and including discharge.

The investigation should be swift, objective and comprehensive. If in the investigation bullying is validated, the bully must be dealt with. Part of the investigation should be an assessment as to whether the bully can be rehabilitated.

If the assessment concludes that the bully cannot change, the bully must be removed from the situation, where they are not able to bully others. If they are moved within the organization, it is important that this move is not seen to be a reward.

If the assessment concludes that the bully can change, the organization should offer to help put a corrective action plan in place and closely monitor the situation.

Case Study—Onto Pleasure Island— Pam's Story

In 2007, Pam was approached by an executive recruiter about an opportunity to join a global pharmaceutical company. Pam considered the executive recruiter to be a friend as they had worked for the same company a number of years earlier. The recruiter's recommendation that this opportunity would be a good fit for Pam was the sole reason why she considered the job.

At the time, Pam was a highly successful executive for another pharmaceutical company. In the ten years she worked for the company, she had been promoted six times. Prior to this, Pam spent six years as a top performer in the packaged goods industry with a company she joined after graduating from university.

After the initial meeting with the executive recruiter, Pam met with the company's CEO, Karl, on a number of occasions, and Ellen the EVP of Human Resources. Pam had some reservations about taking the position, as she had heard from outside people that she trusted that the CEO was difficult to work for. Some even described him as a bully. Pam talked to the executive recruiter who assured her the rumours were not true.

Both the executive recruiter and Ellen assured Pam that while Karl was very direct, he was a fantastic leader, a visionary, very ethical and fostered a real team spirit.

Had Pam done more research before hiring she would have learned that Karl was, in addition to being the CEO, also the CBO (Chief Bullying Officer) and that the company had many of the characteristics of what I refer to as a "Dictatorial" culture. Pam's story highlights the importance of doing due diligence before deciding to change organizations.

Karl and Ellen were very aggressive in their pursuit of Pam. Karl, Pam later learned, had been overheard saying that he "nabbed a trophy hire" from a competitor.

Pam was offered a compensation package significantly higher than what she was making and a guarantee of a promotion within the first year. These were clear indicators that she was a strategic hire and would be a contender to become Karl's replacement.

Based on what Pam felt was "a deal simply too good to pass up," she accepted the offer.

When Pam joined the company, her first priority was to meet with all the managers in her department. In these meetings most of the managers indicated that there were major cultural issues in the department and that the issues were linked to Nicole, one of Pam's direct reports. There were accusations that Nicole bullied people, both within the department and throughout the organization. The human resource representative for the department provided a background on Nicole and data that showed turnover in the department was high, largely due to Nicole's bullying. There was also an independent mediator's report, which characterized Nicole's leadership within the department like the movies *Mean Girls* and *Lord of the Flies*. Others in the company spoke about a long history of Nicole being constantly combative and pitting her team against others in the company. For some reason she seemed to have been able to do this with impunity.

Almost from the beginning, Pam found that she was being undermined by Nicole and being treated as if she had no authority. Nicole routinely refused to communicate directly with her, publicly refused to attend key meetings and walked out on meetings held by Pam. Pam also became aware that Nicole and Karl met on a regular basis without informing her. Nicole made it clear to Pam that she felt that she was more qualified than Pam to run the department.

In meetings with her peers, Pam learned that there was a lot of speculation that Karl and Nicole were having an affair, which was commonly known within the company and across the industry. The speculation gained some credibility with Pam when she, Karl and Nicole went on a field trip. Pam drove and Karl and

Nicole ignored her the entire day. At the end of the day, Karl and Nicole went out for dinner without inviting Pam.

Pam went to Ellen for advice. Ellen went to great lengths to assure Pam that there was no merit in the speculation, that she had spoken to Karl about it and he acknowledged that he and Nicole had a strong working relationship, but it did not go beyond that. Ellen's advice was for Pam to meet with Nicole and confront her on the behavioral issues.

Pam met with Nicole, who reacted badly and insisted that a meeting be held with her, Karl, Ellen and Pam.

Pam agreed with this and a meeting was held the next day.

At this meeting Karl and Ellen clearly wanted to appease Nicole, complimenting her on her performance and suggesting that her passion and dedication caused her to behave the way she did. Nicole agreed that this was the case, but claimed she did not mean to offend anyone and that while she was disappointed in not getting Pam's position, she wanted to support her nonetheless.

Pam wanted to reach an understanding that if Nicole was going to meet with the CEO, that she be made aware of it, and the CEO would not form a judgment or make a decision based on one-sided information. This was agreed. But Pam didn't feel relieved. She walked away from the meeting with her worst fears confirmed. Ellen and Karl were trying to pacify both Nicole and Pam. Nothing changed. Nicole continued to walk out of meetings with Pam, sent her out-dated marketing reports to present at meetings, bullied Pam's employees and had private meetings with Karl.

Almost immediately after the meeting Karl started going after Pam with a litany of tactics designed to set her up for failure, including suggesting that Pam was leaking internal information to a competitor (which is what Karl did with a number of people he targeted as a rationale to get them out). Other tactics included leaving her out of key communications, making decisions in her area without informing her, leaving her out of key reports and emails to the management committee and continuing to deal directly with Nicole.

Pam now had no doubt that she was in trouble, but had no idea what to do. It seemed like a bad dream. Her life and career had been so on track just six months earlier. Remember Honest John and Gideon tempting the children away from school and onto Pleasure Island with promises of untold amusement and treats? But not a hint of what happened to the children there—Pam could relate.

Pam went to a number of peers for advice. While all of them were sympathetic, none wanted to get involved because they were afraid of Karl and none of them trusted Ellen. Pam learned that earlier in the year, five people went to the Board of Directors expressing ethical concerns they had about Karl, including their speculation about his affair with Nicole.

The situation was taking a serious toll on Pam's health. She was unable to sleep and began losing weight. The situation was so unreal and unjust that she constantly wondered if she had done something to deserve this. Pam had no one to confide in within the company. Her relationships with friends and family became increasingly strained. Pam finally sought professional help and was diagnosed with Post Traumatic Stress Disorder.

Pam then went for legal advice. The lawyer advised her to file for constructive dismissal, which she did, and negotiate a severance package. She left the company a broken woman with no allies, including the executive recruiter, whom she firmly believes knew what Karl was like. The executive recruiter would no longer even return her calls.

The story does not end here. A few months later, Pam landed another position. She received a glowing six-month review with a comment on how well she fit into the workplace culture. A couple of weeks after the review her new CEO requested an introduction to Karl so that he could make a sales pitch. Pam facilitated the introduction. Less than twenty-four hours after facilitating the introduction, the CEO fired Pam, saying she was a "poor fit." There was no question in Pam's mind that Karl had discredited her to the CEO and Karl made doing business with them conditional on Pam being fired.

Fortunately, because Pam was highly regarded in the industry and had a solid track record prior to going to "Pleasure Island" she was able to relocate and is gainfully employed with an organization whose values are more in line with hers. While this is a happy ending for Pam it is unlikely that she will ever fully recover from the horrible experience and will always have to be concerned that Karl will seek further retaliation.

The Board of Directors did confront Karl on the issues brought forward by the five "Whistleblowers" and conducted a cursory investigation (they did not even interview three individuals who could provide specific details on the allegations made—these names were suggested by the whistleblowers). They claim not to have found any wrongdoing. Karl adamantly denied the affair. Even after Karl was caught by a private investigator leaving Nicole's home after spending the night there and the evidence was given to the Board, they still did nothing. Keep in mind that this was in and around the same time frame that the Hewlett Packard Board fired their CEO because of the circumstances around an affair he was alleged to have had with a contract employee.

As time went on, Karl became even bolder in his questionable business practices and in his relationship with Nicole—he was, some suspected, taunting the board into firing him to trigger his "golden parachute."

Four of the five whistleblowers were forced out of the company and found that they were under surveillance. Phones and emails were being monitored before and after they left, and company funds were used for this activity. These people also found that they were "Blacklisted."

Thirteen months after the "cursory" investigation a key group of employees staged a revolt and Karl abruptly resigned.

Author's Note

This case study captures the profile of a CBO—how human resources is culpable and part of the problem and the negligence on the part of the board.

During the course of my career, I have dealt with a large number of boss/subordinate affairs that created problems in the organization. One in particular stands out when a board member challenged me by stating, "This is common place. It's part of human nature." I expressed that I was offended that he thought I was that naive and questioned,

1. "Is it okay for the CEO to breach company policy?"

2. "If he is breaching this policy, is it possible he is breaching other policies?"

3. "If the CEO is exempt from certain policies, how can they be enforced with others?"

4. "Is it okay for the subordinate to receive extreme favoritism because of the relationship?"

5. "Is it okay for the subordinate to abuse her power and bully others because of her access to the CEO?"

6. "Is it okay that the majority of management lost respect and confidence in the CEO?"

I indicated that as in most cases of this nature, "The affair is a secondary issue. It is what happens because of the affair."

Even with my retort, I don't think the board member got it!

Case Study—Alone In a Man's World—Sonya's Story

After graduating from university in 2004, Sonya enrolled in an elite firefighting academy and completed six months of rigorous training. Sonya was the only female in a class of thirty.

After graduating from the academy Sonya joined a fire department in a mid-sized municipality. As in the academy, Sonya was the only female on the force. Initially, the relationship with her Captain and fellow Firefighters was positive.

By the time Sonya had two years in, she had come to know Rob, her Captain, quite well. Sonya was twenty-eight years old at the time and the Captain was fifty-seven. As a Firefighter, it is key to be a team player, and because you are working in such close proximity for long periods of time developing close bonds is critical.

Sonya felt comfortable with Rob and viewed him not only as her superior, but also a mentor. Sonya knew that Rob had taken her under his wing and thought that his interest in her was strictly professional.

Over time Rob's attentions were starting to cross the line. He was giving Sonya a lot of special attention, singling her out for preferred assignments, always trying to sit next to her during meals, calling her on the intercom letting her know he was going to bed, etc. The other firefighters started to notice what was going on and Rob's actions became the fodder for gossip and jokes.

While Rob's attentions were never overt or threatening, they were starting to make Sonya very uncomfortable. There was no question in Sonya's mind that Rob had a crush on her.

Sonya contemplated going to Rob and telling him his attentions were making her uncomfortable. However, she decided against this because she knew from what she had observed that Rob had a mean streak and retaliated against those who crossed him.

Sonya decided that her best option was to go to the Senior Captain and request a transfer to another station. While she did not file a formal complaint, Sonya did tell the Senior Captain the reason for her request. An immediate transfer was arranged.

A few weeks after the transfer Sonya ran into Rob when they were both off duty. In greeting Rob, Sonya was friendly but distant. Rob called her at home that night and demanded to know why she requested the transfer and why she was so distant with him. Sonya indicated to Rob that his call was totally inappropriate and he hung up on her.

The next time Sonya was scheduled to be on duty Sonya was told that Rob was in the Captain's office and wanted to meet with her. Sonya was frightened and refused to meet with him. While Sonya hid upstairs she overheard Rob go into a tirade with her Captain.

From that point, Rob mounted a campaign against Sonya. He was furious that she was rejecting and avoiding him. Although they worked at different locations and she worked for a different Captain, Rob still exercised considerable influence over her. In situations where all stations were called into an emergency, (which is often the case) Sonya was under his command.

Using his cronies, Rob initiated a letter writing campaign. Through coercion he forced firefighters to write to the Senior Captain with fictitious concerns about Sonya's judgment and physical fitness, and that they considered her a safety risk. In addition to sending these "reports" to the Senior Captain, photo copies were widely circulated. When off duty Rob was constantly working the phones encouraging his cronies to find any reason to "write her up."

Sonya recalls a number of occasions she witnessed Rob speaking with her fellow firefighters, pointing in her direction, and walking away shaking his head.

The campaign was working. Sonya was being shunned by her fellow firefighters. They whispered amongst themselves, gave her sideways looks, and head shaking was routine. Almost no one would talk to her and she was excluded from most activities at the station, alone in a man's world!

Sonya also found that her equipment and gear were being tampered with. On one occasion, all of her gear and name tag were removed. When she found her overhead bag she found her name tag along with an open box cutter. Had Sonya just reached into her bag she could have seriously cut herself. Fortunately she was not hurt, but her sense of security was badly shaken. When Sonya reported this to her Captain, he accused her of setting it up to deflect from the concerns he and her fellow Firefighters had regarding her being viewed as a safety risk.

Sonya now felt that not only was her job at risk but also her personal safety. This was reinforced when she ran into Rob at her station and he threatened that something bad would happen if she stayed, and that by staying she was putting everyone she worked with at risk.

This was the breaking point for Sonya, and in November of 2007 she made a formal complaint on the advice of a friend who is a lawyer.

Initially the complaint was filed with the Senior Captain, who referred it to an Assistant Deputy Chief who dealt with workplace harassment, discrimination and abuse issues. The advisor wrote up a report which went directly to the Chief who immediately forwarded it to the city's Director of Human Resources who initiated an investigation.

It was clear to Sonya at the outset that this was the first time that anything like this had occurred in the municipality. The union representing the firefighters initially resisted the investigation and needed to be educated on the legalities involved and the process. This resulted in a delay in getting the process started.

Almost everyone in the squad was interviewed. Most were clearly uncomfortable with it and made it known to Sonya that they did not like it. The fear factor was also at play and they knew that if it got back to Rob that they supported Sonya's claim, he was capable of retaliation. Sonya's isolation from her coworkers got worse, they resented a female junior Firefighter taking on a very senior Captain. Fortunately there were a few who supported Sonya's position, particularly those who had their own experiences with Rob.

Confidentiality became an issue, and it was very obvious to Sonya that there was a lot of talk going on. After people were interviewed they huddled amongst themselves to compare notes.

Sonya was interviewed a number of times during the process and often felt that she was fighting this alone against Rob, her coworkers, the union and to some extent the administration.

During the interviews the Investigator challenged whether Sonya was able to do the work of a Firefighter. The Director of Human Resources offered to move her to another Department. Through all of this Sonya remained resolved.

The investigation took a long 379 days, over a year, to complete. During this period the isolation, fear and anxiety affected her health, requiring her to call in sick thirteen times. Sonya knew when she would not be able to perform as a firefighter, and if there was a fire when she felt this way, she would be a safety risk.

Finally the Investigator completed his report and found that her complaint had merit and the treatment she received was unjust. Included in the report were references to other situations where Rob bullied his subordinates.

By mutual agreement, Rob took early retirement.

Following the Investigator's recommendations, all Departments in the city had a cultural assessment conducted and a number of positive changes were made to ensure that employees were not at risk of being bullied. Everyone went through an extensive awareness program on bullying and everyone in a supervisory position went through an extensive training program on bullying. The city is now considered a model for good leadership and staff relations. Also, there is a much more streamlined process to investigate complaints. Sonya credits the Director of Human Resources for helping her cope through this long ordeal and keeping in touch with her to see how she was doing and also to assure her that the investigation was not forgotten. While the Director of Human Resources should be credited for doing the right thing, the investigation took far too long. Sonya went through sheer hell for over a year—the length of time it took to conduct the investigation!

Author's note

As indicated in the study, although the municipality and the director of human resources did the right things, next to the bullying the big issue here is the bureaucratic culture, where the time it took to resolve worsened an already bad situation. This has often been the case in situations I was brought into. When dealing with a bullying situation, it must be investigated promptly. Many human resource professionals become slaves to the bureaucracy and process becomes a substitute for purpose.

Conducting a Workplace Assessment

Determining "At Risk" Position

The 2012 collapse of the 168-year-old News of the World and the public humiliation of media mogul Rupert Murdoch should give rise to organizational leaders satisfying themselves that their cultures do not put their organizations at risk.

Murdoch's testimony before the British parliamentary committee was in essence an admission that he is totally out of the loop on how his organizations operate. For someone who has long had the reputation of being a hands-on manager, his defense comes across as questionable. While we suspect that Murdoch may have been aware of some of the tactics to get the scoops scored by his newspapers, it is entirely possible that he did not fully understand or appreciate how a culture of fear can destroy an organization and people. While Murdoch places the blame on those he trusted, he and his board should at the very least acknowledge management neglect.

It is my assertion that most organizational leaders do not fully understand or appreciate the power, both positive and negative, of organizational culture.

Many organizational leaders relegate the "cultural stuff" to their human resource people, believing that it is sufficient to have values and operating principles plastered all over the place, rarely assessing whether they are consistently applied and are reflective in the actual culture that exists.

I have found that it usually takes a major incident for organizational leaders to consider bullying as a major risk. In all of the instances where I was called in after a major incident, leaders in the organization were shocked to find that the incident could have been prevented had they paid closer attention to telltale signs that were evident. They were also amazed at how little they really knew about what was going on in their organization.

I encourage organizational leaders to be proactive in identifying the telltale signs and really understand the cultures that they lead and the impacts and risks involved.

To determine the actual culture that exists within an organization requires a comprehensive review of a number of fronts. As all of the fronts are interrelated, reviewing and analyzing them in isolation will not show the whole picture. Connecting this analysis with cultural indicators will yield insights that should capture the attention of even the most hardened and skeptical leader.

When I conduct assessments for organizations I go below the surface, helping organizational leaders gain information that may not be obvious or not brought to their attention. I look for undisclosed workplace cultural issues and connect seemingly unrelated comments, events and situations to identify the risks and opportunities.

The assessment process has four stages that are customized based on individual organizational needs.

The four stages are as follows:

Stage 1

Documentation and Program Review

I review and assess the effectiveness of the organizations:

- Policies and procedures
- Definition of workplace bullying and violence

- Employee surveys and their robustness
- Employee complaints
- Past incidents reports
- Employment programs
- Incident investigations

Stage 2

Analyzing the Fronts

This stage involves gaining a comprehensive interview-based understanding of the workplace. Employees at various levels are interviewed with assurances of confidentiality to determine workplace dynamics and the strengths and weaknesses of the organizational structure. This is where I delve into the eleven fronts:

- Governance
- Structure
- Decision making
- Politics
- Systems and technology
- Communication
- Roles and responsibilities
- Accountabilities
- Measurements
- Rewards and recognition
- Alignment

Stage 3

Cultural Indicators

A review and analysis of a number of cultural indicators will help identify the impacts that culture has on the individual and the organization. The indicators are:

- Staff turnover—overall organization—by department—by employee category.

- Run rate vacancies by department—by employee category.

- Absentee rate, short and long term—by department—by employee category.

- Stress leave experience.

- Frequency and severity of workplace accidents.

- History of suicides or attempted suicides.

- Participation rate of people using a employee assistance program EAP.

- Proportion of internal promotions to external hires for positions beyond entry level.

- Termination rate (i.e. those who are fired)—overall organization—by department.

- Resignation rate—overall organization—by department.

- Reasons people cite for leaving.

- History of grievances or complaints.

- History of human rights claims filed.

- Activity on whistleblower hot line or other vehicles used to report wrongdoings.

Stage 4

Report and Recommendations

In my final stage, I present the outcome of the assessment process:

- Identification of risk behaviors in the organization.
- A fear factor gauge.
- Report on the impact of existing systems, processes and practices.
- Recommendations for creating a sustainable, integrated anti bullying program.
- Baseline from which to annually measure improvement.

Benefits of conducting a comprehensive workplace assessment:

1. Provides senior management with the organization's risk profile.
2. Determines the prevalence of incidents and a baseline from which to track trending of risk profile.
3. Identifies areas of highest risk within the overall organization which assists in prioritizing changes and interventions.
4. Satisfies legislative compliance requirements.
5. Provides a unique insight in what is really going on in an organization.

Whether an organization resembles a large public enterprise such as Murdoch's News of the World or a small, privately run manufacturing or consulting concern, its leaders require an appreciation of the risks created from workplace culture. The damages arising to individuals, brand, and, indeed, enterprise, from a culture of intimidation, fear and bullying is as significant to an organization's well-being as those risks reviewed regularly by corporate accountants, lawyers and risk managers. I believe that a responsible board of directors and/or executive management team will benefit enormously from the heightened awareness of culture that assessment process reveals. Where an organization's culture and operational systems are positive, transparent and predictable, its employees, customers and shareholders will reward it with positive activities of their own.

Unions And Bullying

In 1972 I began my career as a management labor relations officer in a Chrysler plant in Windsor Ontario, Canada. There I learned—by total immersion—conflict management. Mildly put, the environment was toxic, and barbarically tribal. Most of my time and energy was preventing fist fights between workers and foremen (pretty scary for a 140 lb twenty-three-year-old) and encouraging everyone in the plant from the supervisor to the janitor to be more delicate in their language.

My experience with unions also includes a ten-year stint as chief spokesman for Loblaw, Canada's largest retail food chain—which at the time was 90 percent unionized.

A few decades ago unions were necessary in protecting the rights and representing the interests of workers. It is safe to say that during the recent economic downturn, all too many employees have been and are exploited. Given this, it is perplexing that during this period union membership in the private sector has and continues to decline.

The reasons for the decline can easily be rationalized by blaming Right to Work Legislation in some states, the most recent being Michigan, reactions by management to organizing drives by bullying employees with the threat of closing or moving their operations offshore and targeting employees who are considered ring leaders.

In situations where I have been brought in to consult management on organizing drives, most executives' first instinct is to kill the drive at any cost. When I question why their employees feel it necessary to be represented, the reaction is usually hostile silence.

There is no question that legislation and fear factor are valid explanations for the reason unionized labor is on the decline.

Valid as they may be, there is a much bigger factor—that is how unions are viewed by workers. The prevailing view among union workers is that unions bully their members into doing (or not doing) things that conflict with their interests, values and beliefs.

According to the US National Labor Relations Board website, in 2010 there were 6,000 charges against unions for violating labor laws mostly relating to union attempts to restrain employees from exercising their rights. This number like other Human Rights complaints is likely lower because of the fear factor in reporting.

An example is in Ontario, Canada, in 2013 when teachers were bullied into withdrawing from extracurricular activities as an act of protest because the legislated inability to strike— the withdrawal of the extracurricular was a form of "work to rule."

A large contingent of teachers did not support this action because it went against their professional philosophy. Notwithstanding their objections, most complied with the "work to rule out of fear." It takes a lot of courage to go against the union in situations like this because those who do will likely be viewed and treated as traitors forever by the die-hards and the union leaders.

Unions over the years have evolved to become social activists and a major lobbying force which in many cases is for admirable causes. Some of this activism, however, is in conflict with the interests, values and beliefs of their members, and union leaders have not responded well to the changing diversity of the membership and still are far too rigid in the whole concept that "if you are a brother or sister—there is solidarity."

Solidarity is important for any association or organization; however, when it becomes absolute and enforced through bullying it is no different than what I describe as a Dictatorial Culture.

Case Study—Who Does My Union Represent?—Patrick's Story

Patrick was a city planner for a large North American city. He was one of twenty-six planners and they were represented by a union for municipal employees. Until he was discharged in 2010, Patrick had been with the city for fifteen years.

In July of 2009 the city approached the union for concessions to help reduce a major deficit. The union held a meeting with their members to review this. At the meeting Patrick indicated that the planning department was operating well under their capacity. This is something that Patrick had brought forward to his manager on a number of occasions, usually when a planner left and when they were recruiting for a replacement. Patrick's view was that he and the other planners could process double what they were doing. Every time he raised this with his manager, Patrick was told that the work load was negotiated with the union and to change this would be impossible. After the meeting, Doug, the union representative, asked him, "Are you crazy? *Never,* and I repeat, *never* raise this again!" Patrick fought back by indicating that the city was in trouble and needed to find ways to reduce costs and as a loyal employee he felt obligated to express his views. "In fact," he added, "I know in speaking with people in most departments, there are the same opportunities to reduce costs throughout the organization." Doug told Patrick it was not his place to offer solutions.

Patrick was disturbed by the reaction he got and decided to prove his point. Starting the next day he was able to process the daily assignments by noon, and requested additional assignments.

Patrick's manager refused to do this, on the grounds that doing this would be in violation of the collective agreement.

Not being satisfied with this, Patrick went to the director of Human Resources and was told the same thing, and was advised to "just leave it alone." Prior to this meeting, Patrick reviewed the collective agreement and could find no reference to work load. When he challenged the director on this, she indicated that it was an "unwritten understanding."

For two months, Patrick finished his assignments by noon, without exerting himself. During this period he constantly checked with his manager to have his work reviewed to make sure quality was not compromised. The manager indicated that she was satisfied with the quality of work.

Doug, the union representative, was told by a coworker of Patrick's actions. Doug called Patrick and warned him that if he did not stop, his job would be at risk. Patrick responded by telling Doug that he was not doing anything wrong; in fact what he was doing was the right thing to do to help the city improve their finances. Patrick also made the argument that it was the union's responsibility to find ways to help the city, thereby protecting jobs.

Almost every day after this, Patrick started to receive anonymous threatening emails and calls to his home. The response from the director of Human Resources to his complaint was, "I warned you; you brought this on yourself and there is nothing we can do to help you."

Concurrent with the threatening emails and calls, Patrick's manager started to write Patrick up for poor quality work. At a disciplinary meeting Patrick produced a record of the times he asked his manager to assess the quality of the work and each time he received a positive review. The manager rationalized by indicating she had taken a closer look at the work. Doug also attended the meeting and advised Patrick that he had to support the manager and if the quality of work did not improve, the union would not be able to protect him. Patrick requested that an independent third party be brought in to assess his work. The request was denied. Patrick also requested that an investigation be done on the threatening emails and calls. This request was also denied and he was accused of being the instigator of the emails and calls.

Not one to give up, Patrick went to the police to report the emails and calls. An investigation was conducted. Doug and Patrick's coworkers were questioned. The investigation was inconclusive and Patrick was told that the only thing the Police could do was keep the file on record.

The emails, calls and poor reviews continued for the next few months.

In January of 2010 Patrick was fired for poor performance, and his salary and benefits were immediately terminated. The union did not file a grievance.

In March Patrick suffered a major heart attack and went through a triple bypass operation. Now that he is recovering from this, he is legally challenging the union for failing to represent him and he is filing a civil wrongful dismissal case against the city.

Part Two

The Dynamics of Bullying

"There is exploitation when the Master considers
the Worker not as an associate, as a helper,
but as an instrument from which he must draw
the greatest service at the lowest possible cost.
The exploitation of man by man is slavery."

—Frederic Ozanam

What Exactly Is Bullying?

I n the work that I have done on bullying in the workplace and the interviews conducted during the course of writing this book, I am amazed at the lack of understanding and awareness on the topic, as well as the myths and misinterpretations out there.

The Dignity at Work Campaign in the UK defines workplace bullying as, "Persistent, offensive, abusive, intimidating, malicious or insulting behavior, abuse of power or unfair penal sanctions, which makes the recipient feel upset, threatened, humiliated or vulnerable, which undermines their self confidence and which may cause them to suffer stress."

Profile of a Bully

As we have witnessed with the Lance Armstrong debacle, bullying is all about power, control, deceit, deflection, discrediting, destruction and denial.

For over a decade Armstrong was considered to be "The Boss" of the ICU—"The International Cycling Union" and he had total control over the doping culture of the US (Postal Service) team. In essence he was the Chief Bullying Officer of the sport.

Armstrong bullied to:

- force teammates to use banned substances
- retaliate against those who took an anti-doping stance
- force out of the team those who did not comply
- force out of the team those who testified against him

- discredit those who went against him
- keep people in the know from exposing him
- influence the ICU

In a *60 Minutes* interview Scott Pelly asked the US Anti-doping Agency (USADA) CEO Travis Tigart what Armstrong could do to those who testified against him. Tigart's response was that Armstrong would "Incinerate" anyone who went against him. Tigart himself was bullied and received an anonymous death threat during the course of the investigation he was conducting.

Armstrong's behaviours, demeanor and comments made in various interviews exposed him as a classic narcissistic bully. The Diagnostic and Statistical Manual of Mental Disorders IV classifies those who have a narcissistic disorder as "those who:

- are preoccupied with fantasies of unlimited success;
- believe that they are special and unique;
- require excessive admiration;
- possess a strong sense of entitlement;
- exploit others and lack empathy;
- exhibit high levels of arrogance."

My experience in dealing with bullies—particularly those who have power and control—is that they generally exhibit these narcissistic characteristics. Many are psychopaths and it may well be determined that Armstrong is one (see "Is There A Psychopath In The House?"). People with these disorders are dangerous and responsible for much of the violence in the workplace.

Bullying in the workplace is violence in the workplace. Most organizational leaders have difficulty in identifying it in those terms, which I assert is the major reason that bullying is condoned and in many situations encouraged, and in many organizations even expected of their managers.

The Dynamics of Bullying

David Beale and Helge Hoel in "Workplace Bullying: Industrial Relations and the Challenge for Management in Britain and Sweden," reported that, "Very often, in 70 to 80 percent of the cases, the main culprit occupies a supervisory role while the target is a subordinate."

This is consistent with research done in North America. Coworkers also bully, but they are usually bystanders who in many instances become complicit in the bullying.

The Dignity at Work Campaign in the UK offers the following as some of the most common ways that bullies torment their targets.

"Bullies may:

- Use terror tactics, open aggression, threats, shouting, abuse and obscenities towards their target.

- Subject their target to constant humiliation or ridicule, belittling their efforts, often in front of others.

- Subject their target to excessive supervision, monitoring everything they do and being excessively critical of minor things.

- Take credit for other people's work but never take the blame when things go wrong.

- Override the person's authority.

- Remove whole areas of work responsibility from the person, reducing their job to routine tasks that are well below their skills and capabilities.

- Set for the person what they know to be impossible objectives, or constantly change the work requirement without telling the person, and then criticize or reprimand the person for not meeting their demands.

- Ostracize and marginalize their target, dealing with a person only through a third party, excluding the person from discussions, decisions etc.

- Spread malicious rumours about the individual.

- Refuse reasonable requests for leave, training etc., or block a person's promotion."

Based on the many cases I have worked on, the following also could apply:

- Unreasonably delaying to approve or reject plans or objectives.

- Not providing constructive feedback.

- Making negative comments about the target to others.

- Dealing directly with the target's subordinates and ordering the subordinate not to disclose.

The Five Forms of Bullying

There are five kinds of bullying: verbal, psychological, physical, cyber and blacklisting. While there are many similarities to bullying in schools, there are as many if not more differences—the main one being, bullying by children and pre-adults is far more overt whereas bullying in the workplace is far more calculated in the method by which the bully bullies.

In the workplace a combination of verbal, psychological and cyber bullying is more commonly applied—where in schools it is more of a combination of verbal, cyber and physical, or the threat of physical violence.

In schools bullies use cyber bullying to discredit or embarrass or "out" their targets. The same applies to the workplace; however, it is more extensively used by the bully boss who does it under the guise of performance management.

My direct experience with being targeted was after exposing a corrupt executive. For well over a year I was subject to a combination of psychological, cyber, and (if you include a death threat as physical bullying) physical bullying in retaliation for blowing the whistle. My phones were tapped, my emails were hacked, I was called a "f—ing faggot" in a public forum and for a period of time put under surveillance. When I reported this, the board of directors chose to believe the executive, and only when I produced documented evidence did they start to believe me.

Verbal Bullying

"People who are brutally honest get more
satisfaction out of the brutality than the honesty."

—Richard J Needham

It is very easy for a bully, especially on a one-on-one basis, to verbally abuse a target and is therefore the most common form of bullying. The bully usually rationalizes or defends the behaviors as "just kidding," or "I did not mean to offend, it is just my style," or "I lash out because of my passion," or "it's my way of getting people to produce more."

Psychological Bullying

"Calumny requires no proof. The throwing out of
malicious imputations against any character leaves a stain
which no after-refutation can wipe out. To create an

unfavourable impression, it is not necessary that certain things should be true, but that they have been said."

—William Hazlitt

Bullies are masters of deflection and manipulation who usually set their targets up to emotionally destroy them, which they know will have an effect on the target's performance attendance and attitude, which in turn gives the bully the ammunition to get rid of them.

Psychological bullying is the most difficult form of bullying to deal with. It is usually not just one comment, situation or event, it is a combination of things, well thought out by the bully. When things start seeming out of the norm, it is important to tie seemingly unrelated comments, events and situations together.

Physical Bullying

"Violence is, essentially, a confession of ultimate inarticulateness."

—Time Magazine

Physical violence is more common in the school yard than in the workplace. However, when you add the threat of physical violence it becomes more common.

A September 2012 *Forbes* article by Meghan Casserly called "When Snitches Get Stitches-Physical Violence As Workplace Retaliation On The Rise" reported that "The number one weapon used at work is the fist." This according to Larry Barton, a former professor at Harvard Business School and a leading expert on workplace violence. Barton estimates that more than 1.2 million Americans where physically assaulted in 2011.

According to the American Nurses Association, "The healthcare sector leads all other industries, with 45 percent of all non fatal attacks against workers resulting in lost work days in the US" (BLC, 2006).

Hazing is also a form of physical bullying which does not receive the exposure it should. Targets of this are usually new hires or workers that others consider different in some way. Being the target of this type of aggression is perhaps the most humiliating experience that one can face in the workplace and in all too many environments considered harmless fun.

Cyber Bullying

In today's world cyber bullying has grown to the extent that it is now considered to be a major category of bullying. I assert that most bullies are cowards and the technologies have given many the opportunities to be brave. According to the United States National Crime Prevention Council, cyber bullying occurs "when the Internet, cell phones or other devices are used to send or post texts or images intended to hurt or embarrass another person."

Bully managers use email to harass their target and rationalize it as an effective form of performance management. One individual I interviewed received emails from her boss every day including weekends and holidays, at all hours, day and night, for over two years, and in each instance demanded an immediate response. In many instances, the intent of the emails from bullies is to provoke an angry response from the target. Another means is to entrap them into "The Bully's Trap." Chat rooms and anonymous emails are being used more and more to gossip about and discredit targets.

Blacklisting

In many instances the bullying does not stop after the target leaves. It is a small world and when the target is in the bully's trap the bully continues to discredit the target. In the interviews I conducted, most like Vera in "Vera's Story", who left had great difficulty in getting re-established. I am astonished by the naivety of the so-called professionals who advise people who are targeted to quit, not realizing that the bully usually follows the target, making it almost impossible to get out of the trap.

The Dynamics of Bullying At Play

As you have seen in Vera's story and will see in the other stories—bullies are masters of deflection who usually discredit their targets to the point the target becomes the villain—they usually (in what Stanford Engineering School Management Professor and *Good Boss, Bad Boss* author Robert Sutton has labelled) "kiss up and kick down"—and because they are seen as high producers they are viewed as the heroes who garner more credibility than the target.

Part One deals with the organizational dynamics of bullying, and as you will see in the case studies, the following organizational characteristics are at play:

- A dictatorial or a disjointed culture
- A culture that rewards the bully and blames the target
- Practices that encourage individualism more than team
- A culture where power is vested without checks and balances.

Also in the stories you will see a pattern that is usually evident in bullying:

- A triggering event which is usually a comment, criticism, challenge or action that the bully takes exception to. The trigger could also be the bully viewing the target as a threat.
- The bully's resolve to punish the target.

- The bully's actions
- The bystanders become complicit.
- The target falls into the bully's trap.
- If caught the bullies deflect by turning the target into the culprit.
- The target is reprimanded, gets fired or quits.
- The bully identifies the next target.
- In all too few instances bystanders become witnesses and defenders.
- In even rarer instances the targets take steps to challenge the bully.
- When the target leaves it is difficult to find alternative employment.

Making Distinctions

A point of view can be a dangerous luxury when
substituted for insight and understanding.
—Marshall McLuhan, The Gutenberg Galaxy

Much of this book describes and illustrates what bullying is. One of the most frequent push backs I get, particularly from people who are in management, is the fear that by raising the awareness of bullying, employees will use it as a shield or a sword and that it will restrict managers from being able to do their jobs out of fear they will be labeled as a bully. It is therefore necessary to be clear and make distinctions on what does and what does not constitute bullying.

Disagreements and conflict is a normal dynamic that occurs in all environments. It would be wrong to label all disagreements and conflicts as bullying. It is healthy to raise and debate differing views, as long as it is done in an open, honest, and direct way, and resolved—even if the resolution is to "agree to disagree." Not only is it healthy to have these debates—I assert it is essential to bring differences out in the open, rather than have them fester.

When disagreements or opposing viewpoints are stifled or the parties involved are constantly battling, bullying is likely at play.

To determine what bullying is and what it is not, the following distinctions should be made:

- Cautioning is not bullying, badgering is.
- Coaching is not bullying, humiliating is.
- Disciplining is not bullying, destroying is.

- Competition is not bullying, unhealthy competition is.
- Setting consequences is not bullying, making threats is.
- Holding people accountable is not bullying, seeking revenge is.
- Joking is not bullying, taunting is.
- Flirting is not bullying, stalking is.
- Being tough is not bullying, being mean is.
- Building endurance is not bullying, hazing is.

Cautioning vs. Badgering

Bullying should not be used as a sword or a shield. Managers who properly caution employees on performance, attitude or behavioral issues should not fear being labeled a bully.

Good bosses set high expectations and hold employees accountable for their performance, actions and behaviors. It is not bullying when expectations are clear, reasonable, attainable and fair, and employees are provided with the necessary resources, communication and support to achieve their goals. Bosses can be demanding and tough—that should not necessarily label them a bully.

Bosses who set unreasonable and unattainable expectations, and withhold resources, communications and support are bullies. Usually they use harassment and badger people to perform—this is a form of exploitation and is bullying.

Disciplining vs. Destroying

Part of effective performance management is taking disciplinary action up to and including discharge. When this action is taken with the intent to improve performance or correct behaviors or actions it is not bullying. When this action is taken to set up a target it becomes bullying. When targets fall into the bully's trap they give the bully the ammunition they need to take disciplinary action—not to correct, but as you have read in Vera's story, to destroy.

Throughout my career I have had to invite many people out of the organizations I have worked with. Dismissing an employee is one of the most difficult things a manager has to do. In taking this action it is critical to maintain the person's dignity. It never fails to amaze me how people are destroyed, not so much by this final act but the method by which the action is taken. In August of 2013 when AOL Chief Tim Armstrong publicly fired Alel Lenz, the creative director of Patch (a division on AOL) on the spot when Armstrong was addressing the unit's 1,100 employees, a new standard on how not to dismiss employees was established.

Coaching vs. Humiliating

To most readers, the misrepresentation will be quite obvious. A manager who publicly chastises an employee in front of coworkers, emphasizing everything negative about the employee's performance, may defend himself with an assertion that he was coaching the employee. However, the bystanders and the target will probably perceive it for what it is—humiliation—and nothing more. Nothing has been taught, no coaching has taken place. The only result is bad feelings for everyone involved. The differences between coaching and humiliating are obvious. Even professional coaches can fall into this trap, heaping insult onto injury after a defeat. However, when true coaching wins over humiliation the differential between gains and losses is enormous.

A Separation Label

Early in my career I had the benefit of having a coach who influenced my management and leadership philosophy for life.

Bob McCutcheon, a senior executive at Loblaw Companies Limited (Canada's largest food retailer), appeared in my office early one morning, sat down and took out his pipe (they allowed smoking in those days).

As he prepared his pipe (a long, drawn-out process) he started. "Son I have a major problem. You see, there is a young manager; he is cocky, overly aggressive to the point of being abrasive, not sensitive to others, unreasonably demanding, doesn't listen to others, and bullies people to get things done. I'm totally perplexed on what to do." Flattered that Bob, who was considered the senior statesman, would come to me with such a weighty issue, I quickly said, "I would fire the SOB." After taking a long drag from his pipe Bob responding by saying, "Well, son, that's my dilemma. You're the SOB I am talking about."

Thankfully Bob did not follow the advice, but for me it was a lifelong coaching lesson and I went on to become at age twenty-nine the youngest vice president with the organization and enjoyed a twenty-three-year career with them.

Competition vs. Unhealthy Competition

Like conflict, competition is a fact of life. We live in a competitive society and it is not altogether a bad thing. Some competition is healthy and some is not.

Healthy competition celebrates excellence on either side. Healthy competition is motivated out of a love of the game or task, whatever it may be, and doing it well.

Bullying is often at play in unhealthy competition. In unhealthy competition, beating others or being the best is the only goal, and the pressure to win is more important than the fun of playing or learning skills. Unhealthy competition celebrates victory over others, sometimes at any cost. Unhealthy competition is motivated out of a fear of losing.

How employees are measured, rewarded, recognized, and advanced influences both healthy and unhealthy competition. For example team goals, metrics, and rewards foster healthy competition, but with heavily weighted individual goals, metrics and rewards, the risk of unhealthy competition is there. Also pitting employees against each other creates a risk of unhealthy competition.

An example of healthy competition in the workplace would be one in which two teams faced off to solve the same problem. At the end of the competition the teams come together and share their solutions and processes. Competition like this can lead to startling innovation as teams share and learn from each other and lift each other up at the same time.

An example of unhealthy competition in the workplace would be groups or individuals pitted against each other for the approval of a boss. The two sides grow defensive of each other and focus on undermining each as communication breaks down. Feelings of acrimony, hostility, and contempt are planted and the groups employ destructive tactics like sabotage, gossip, and innuendo. They malign each other on the company intranet, and the efforts of the entire department suffer as a result.

An infamous illustration of unhealthy competition is the incident between U.S. Olympic Figure Skating teammates Tonya Harding and Nancy Kerrigan. In January of 1994, in a nefarious display of unhealthy competition, figure skating champion Nancy Kerrigan was literally taken out at the knees by the husband of her rival Tonya Harding, eliminating Kerrigan from the 1994 U.S. Figure Skating Championship. Tonya Harding was subsequently disgraced, and after contests with alcohol and impaired driving charges, she took her demons into the ring by launching a female boxing career, just as Lance Armstrong has brought unhealthy competition to a whole new level.

Holding Accountable vs. Seeking Revenge

People should be held accountable for their words, actions, behaviors and performance. When retaliatory action is taken it becomes revenge.

Consequences vs. Threats

There are good and bad consequences—to outline what could occur in the event or as a result of an action or behavior is not bullying. When threats are used, e.g., "If you don't do this, you will be fired," it is bullying. An example of outlining a consequence is: "Breach of this policy could result in disciplinary action, up to and including discharge."

Joking vs. Taunting

The workplace should be a fun place to be. It is okay to poke fun at someone, and it is even more effective if you poke fun at yourself. Joking and teasing has to be a give and take—simply put, if you can't take it, don't give it.

One time inappropriate and offensive comments said in jest are not bullying; it becomes bullying when the comments are repeated and used to offend, disparage, insult, demean and ridicule.

In Palm Beach in 2012, a former police captain challenged his demotion to an officer. Two officers claimed that the captain created a hostile work environment by using slurs against women, Jews, racial minorities, gays, and people who are overweight. The offensive behavior is alleged to have occurred over a period of years and six people have lodged discrimination and harassment complaints.

The captain's defense is that he was only joking and he has a "strong sense of humor." A witness in his defense claimed, "He's a jovial and joking kind of guy. I've seen people go back and forth, but it is always smiles." It should be noted that this witness was not a target and the people who were did not see the humor.

During my career I have dealt with a number of similar situations, and in most cases the person accused rationalizes the behaviors as "just joking—did not mean to be harmful or malicious," and in all of these cases I found that they were guilty of bullying with the intent to hurt and harm.

Flirting vs. Stalking

Flirting is part of human nature, and it would be wrong and impossible to make it illegal in the workplace. Stalking is harassing, with unwanted and obsessive attention. There is a line when flirting starts to become bullying. That line is when it becomes unwanted, and if the flirting continues the stalking begins and it is bullying. Most cases can be easily dealt with by the person who is being flirted with simply by saying something to the effect of, "I am flattered that you are giving me attention, but it is making me uncomfortable." This unfortunately does not always stop it—usually when the person making the advancements has some power or control over the target.

Toughness vs. Meanness

"Nothing is more despicable than respect based on fear."

—Albert Camus

Tough bosses are often accused of being bullies. Those who are tough and mean usually are. By my definition, being tough is setting high but reasonable expectations and holding people accountable for their performance, behaviors, and actions. I consider myself as being a tough boss, and based on feedback received I have garnered the respect of subordinates. The tough bosses who are mean are not respected—they are feared.

On Saturday August 31, 2013, the *New York Times* in an article by Jack Ewing subtitled "Suicide Draw's Attention to a Top Banker's Tough Tactics" reported the suicide of Pierre Wauthier a 53-year-old chief financial officer of the Zurich Insurance Company in Switzerland. Zurich is one of the world's largest insurers. In a note written by Mr. Wauthier shortly before he died, he "blamed pressure from Mr. Ackermann (the Chairman of Zurich) for his despair" and said that Ackermann "was forcefully trying to lift profits".

Mr. Ackermann resigned shortly after Mr. Wauthier's death. Ewing wrote: "Another way to view the story is that Mr. Ackermann was simply a top manager doing what top managers are supposed to do when a company is not performing as well as it should…and that it is possible that his suicide had more to do with personal demons than pressure brought to bear by Ackermann." I predict that many organizational leaders will take this view rather than internalize this tragedy and question whether their tactics could drive someone to such despair.

I challenge this view on the basis that it may well be that Mr. Wauthier was dealing with "personal demons"; however, it must give rise to the question of what created those personal demons? In his own words Mr. Wauthier blamed Ackerman for his despair. As I indicated earlier it is not a question of being tough; it is the method by which results are achieved that is the bullying, not the toughness.

Building Endurance vs. Hazing

In the section "Altering the Attitudes of Organizational Leaders," I use the Miami Dolphins harassment case to illustrate the distinction between building endurance and bullying. Hazing takes place in the workplace usually to initiate a new employee or degrade someone who is or perceived to be different. People who do the hazing rationalize it as harmless fun, which in some cases may be true; however, when the target is degraded in any way through racial or homophobic slurs or forced to conduct disgusting acts the only people who are having any fun are the bullies and, sadly, bystanders.

Bullying and Performance Management

Making Weak Management Strong

Ambiguity and subjectivity in performance management gives managers a license to bully and discredit their subordinates. A host of European studies have found that many of the environmental characteristics that contribute to bullying are actually describing the functional features of a work unit and that most of them are also factors related to leadership style and supervisory practices. Heinz Leymann commented in his article, "The Content and Development of Mobbing at Work," "that of the eight hundred cases studied where mobbing (bullying) occurred frequently, an almost stereotypical pattern of poorly organized working methods and weak management were found." Forcing people out of an organization is the number one motivation that bullies have for targeting their victims. Bullies usually use poor performance and/or a poor attitude to build a case against their target.

Without clear, fair, reasonable and measurable expectations, managers are left to their own devices to manage performance. Where there is a lack of systems to set and measure expectations, there is usually frustration.

Employees are frustrated because they are not sure of what is expected of them or feel they are being taken advantage of if the manager sets unrealistic targets, or uses favoritism in the allocation of work, or uses the lack of a system to set the employee up to fail. This frustration also causes employees attitude to sour.

When this happens, the bystanders or coworkers get frustrated. They are frustrated because they believe or are conditioned to believe that someone is not pulling their weight and if there is a poor attitude they are considered to be a complainer and/or a trouble maker. Where the target falls into *"a trap,"* the bystanders or coworkers usually side with the bully because the bully has proven that his target is a poor performer and/or has a bad attitude.

Without some form of performance management system in place, poor quality managers will become frustrated as well and lash out at people whom they believe are not meeting expectations.

Generally, employees at all levels respond well to clear expectations and enjoy working in high performance organizations. Being part of a winning team is a real motivator. The key to employees accepting, even embracing clear and high expectations is that they be fair and attainable and be measured. Predator bullies, however, resist performance management systems and attempt to manipulate them.

There are various types of systems, including engineered labor standards. It largely depends on the type of operation and nature of work, which type of system is most effective. Most organizations have industry or sector benchmarks, best practice performance management systems, standards and targets available to them.

There is a myth that bullying legislation and/or anti-bullying policies restrict and limit managers from having open and honest conversations with their subordinates and that employees will abuse legislation and policies as a shield or a sword when they are challenged on performance or attitude issues. The reality is without performance management systems in place, organizations are at risk of having employees use legislation and/or policies to lodge complaints that they are being bullied when they are challenged on performance. The other reality is, where there is an effective and fair performance management system in place there are fewer complaints, regardless of legislation or policies that are in place.

Research suggests that overloaded and bullied employees tend to work for organizations that are declining or shrinking, where the management style is bureaucratic and reactive. In contrast, those employees who feel purposeful, energized and recognized are those that work for growing, dynamic companies where the management style is empowering and successful.

With an effective and fair performance management system in place, managers are able to have a positive discussion with their subordinates even when correcting deficiencies. Rather than lashing out, they are able to have a fact-based conversation that addresses what the employee needs to do to meet expectations or targets and how the manager can help them instead of threatening them.

Women Do Not Need to Bully to Break Through the Glass Ceiling

During my career I have mentored a number of women as they advanced to managers and executives. As most organizations are still dominated by males, it is a challenge for women to break through the glass ceiling, and most of the women I have worked with have had to fight their way to the top echelons of management.

Women are conditioned to be tough in order to progress (even survive) in male-dominated organizations. Also in these environments women have to meet higher standards on proving their toughness than their male peers. Again, as indicated earlier, being tough should not be considered to be a negative attribute. It is, however, when it is being tough and mean.

Clearly a double standard exists; when a woman asserts herself, even if she is not a bully, she is very likely going to be called a bitch or be told that she is being emotional. When a man is tough, but not a bully, he usually garners respect and when he bullies, it is usually rationalized as "doing what he has to do to get things done." When women react to comments, situations, or actions they find offensive people may make a comment like, "If you can't take the heat, get out of the kitchen."

Bottom line, women have had to develop a thicker skin than men to advance, and in so doing, often fall into *The Bully's Trap*— in essence becoming a bully who is targeted by another bully.

Again, based on my experience, there is a double standard applied as both male targets of the bullying and organizations are less tolerant when women bully men than vice versa.

A dynamic commonly at play in women bullying women is the motive of eliminating a real or perceived threat. Common ways this is manifested is discrediting through gossip and innuendo or exclusion. I have observed many instances when women who progress in an organization have less talent than some of their subordinates. These women often know they have less talent than the women they are excluding and so view their bullying as the means to keep their positions, both professional and social. Organizations that have implemented affirmative action programs or quotas have often promoted women with less talent than some of their subordinates.

One comment that someone made resonated greatly with women I have spoken to on the topic: "If there are two women in a board meeting and ten men, the two women will view each other as the greatest threat rather than any of the men."

Sexual Bullying

"Welcome sexual harassment is an oxymoron."

—Richard Posner

As there is an abundance of published material on sexual harassment and how it is defined and the impacts, there is no need for me to expand on what already exists. I will rather focus on the dynamics of sexual bullying in the workplace.

Where there is sexual harassment in the workplace, like other forms of bullying, it is usually boss to subordinate and where the person making the advancements has some power or control over the target.

In the many cases of sexual bullying I have dealt with over my career, most were women who were bullied by a boss who believed he was entitled by virtue of the position he held, and often emboldened, knowing the target would be too afraid to report. In most cases, threats or promises were made, and usually sexual favours were sought in exchange for extra pay and/or promotions. While the majority of cases are male bosses bullying female subordinates, male and female bosses also target male subordinates for sexual favours.

Rush Limbaugh the conservative talk show host made a crude comment: "Some of these babes, I'm telling you, like the sexual harassment crowd, they are out there protesting what they actually wish would happen to them," and this reflects an attitude that is far too prevalent in people of power. They assume that people who are subordinate to them as Limbaugh asserts wish for the advances because of who they are. This has been the case in the vast majority of the sexual harassment situations that I have had to deal with during my career.

In August of 2013 Bob Filner resigned as Mayor of San Diego as part of a sexual harassment settlement with his former press secretary Irene McCormack Jackson. After Jackson filed her suit 17 others have come forward accusing harassment, including two women who had been raped while serving in the armed forces. Filner appears to be a serial sexual predator, which I have found to be the case with the majority of the cases I have dealt with. If one person comes forward and it is found to be credible, you can bet that there are many others who have been assaulted by the predator.

On August 22, 2012, the UK *Telegraph* in an article by John-Paul Ford Rojas called "Bullying seen as acceptable in the army" reports that an Adjunct General in a survey he conducted found that every woman questioned was a victim of unwanted attention. The survey interviewed 6,000 of 25,000 under the General's command, and 400 were women.

A US Department of Defense report in 2012 indicated approximately 26,000 members of the military were sexually assaulted, and of these 53 percent were attacks on men where the majority of perpetrators were men who identify themselves as heterosexual. Given the fear and shame factors in reporting, these numbers are understated, and like other forms of bullying it is hard to capture the true scope and dimension of the issue.

Another dynamic of sexual bullying is the bully who retaliates the target for rejecting his or her advances. This is one of the biggest reasons targets are afraid to report—rejecting an advance is seen as a career-limiting move. The term "Hell hath no fury like a woman scorned" applies as much to men as it does women. I can relate to this as I have been the target of someone being vindictive because I rejected her advances, and it is one of the most disturbing experiences I have ever encountered.

◦◦◦

An example of how difficult it is for targets to report is that of Virginia Messick, one of sixty-two trainees who were victims of assault or other improper conduct by thirty-two instructors in 2011 at Lackland Air Force Base in San Antonio, Texas.

Virginia did not initially report being raped because the protocol for reporting required that she report it to the person who attacked her.

Case Study—The Ethic of Reciprocity— Linda's Story

Linda is a single mother who has worked as an Administrative Assistant for a Not For Profit Agency for twelve years. Linda's boss, Eric, is the Executive Director who joined the agency five years ago at age sixty-five after retiring as a senior executive with a major pharmaceutical firm.

Eric and Linda enjoyed an excellent working relationship and Eric was always sensitive and responsive to the pressures that Linda faced as a single mom and always accommodated her when she needed to come in late or leave early to attend to her daughter.

Although Linda earned a decent wage, money was tight, she had a mortgage on a condo she bought a few years ago, her car was nine years old and repair costs were starting to cost more than it was worth. Linda's ex is a dead beat and has not provided any financial support since they separated.

In late 2007 Linda was diagnosed with cancer. The prognosis was good; however, she required an operation and the drug regiment required her to be absent from work at least a week a month for eight to twelve months.

Linda's benefits with the agency did not include short-term disability and the drug therapy prescribed was not of the formulary of the medical plan she purchased. Linda felt that there were few options. None of her family members had the capacity to support her through this, nor could her friends. Perhaps if she went to them they could all chip in and collect enough to cover her, but she was not optimistic.

Desperate, Linda went to Eric and laid out the situation. Eric responded immediately by telling her not to worry, he would figure something out. "Your main focus has to be on getting better," he assured her.

The next day Eric told her that she could take off as much time as she needed, with pay, and the agency would pay for her drug therapy, and if she required home care or someone to take care of her daughter while she was being treated, the agency would pay for this as well. Linda was so relieved that she jumped up and gave Eric a big hug.

In early 2008 the tumor was successfully removed and she started the therapy. The side effects were relatively moderate, yet it did require that she be off work for six or seven days after each treatment.

During this period, Eric was wonderful. He not only delivered on his promises, he supported Linda emotionally as well, always asking how she was feeling, inquiring how her daughter was coping and telling her if there was anything else she needed, all she had to do was ask.

In March of 2008 Eric invited Linda out for dinner to discuss the agenda for the next board meeting. That Thursday they had dinner at the Ruth Chris Steakhouse that was located near their office. After going over the agenda for the meeting they exchanged stories about their background, families and friends. Eric confided that his marriage of forty-seven years was not a happy one and he was very lonely for companionship. When they went to their cars, Eric asked Linda if they could meet for dinner on a regular basis. While this raised a bit of a red flag with Linda, she agreed, thinking, "It's the least I can do after everything he has done for me."

For the next few weeks Eric and Linda had dinner except for the weeks that she was in treatment. Even though Eric was old enough to be her father, Linda quite enjoyed his company. He was caring, witty and had the energy of a man twenty years his junior.

In May, Eric indicated that he would be attending a conference in Atlanta and invited Linda along. "It will be good for your professional development." Linda thought it was unusual for Eric to make the hotel arrangements, but once they arrived, she found out why. Checking in Linda was aghast that Eric only made arrangements for one room they had to share. Once they got into the room Linda objected. Eric became irritated and said, "You don't have a choice here. Have you never heard of the ethic of reciprocity?" Linda was upset and confused "What do you mean?" she asked. "Let's face it, I am helping you and now you are going to help me," Eric answered. He continued by saying "You have a choice here, you can leave, but if you do, it's over, I will fire you."

It started that day. Linda had to submit to Eric's demands to save her job and continue to receive financial support for her condition. If she did not have her daughter to think about she would have walked out. Linda also realised that given the overall economic situation and her medical condition she would not be able to find another job.

For a man in his early seventies Eric had an insatiable appetite for sex and he became increasingly demanding, insisting that they get together at a sleazy motel at least twice a week. Linda's only reprieve was when she was in therapy. Even then he tried to convince her to meet. Also, Eric's tastes went from vanilla to kink.

This went on until November of 2009. Linda was at the breaking point. A number of times she almost called the Chair of the Board of the agency but decided against it as Eric and the

Chair were very close and Eric indicated that if she told anyone he would claim that she initiated "the affair."

In the last week of November Eric drove Linda to a new location. They went into a building that looked like a warehouse. Once they got inside Linda discovered that it was a sex club. In the center of the room was a huge mattress with a number of people engaged in all kinds of revolting activities. "Here is the deal," Eric said, "we are going to check our clothing in the locker room, then I want you to join in the group, while I watch."

Linda had had enough, and she ran to the entrance and got out. Fortunately she was able to grab a cab and asked the driver to take her home. Once she got home Linda called the police who came over immediately.

Eric was charged with sexual assault and his case is still pending. The Board of Directors asked for and received his resignation.

Linda continues to work for the agency. Eric's replacement is a former Board member and she and Linda have a good working relationship. Being a cancer survivor, the new Executive Director was able to relate to what Linda was going through medically; however, she like others could not imagine the horror Linda suffered by following Eric's distorted view of the "ethic of reciprocity."

Sexual Orientation and Bullying in the Workplace

"Keeping executives from coming out are
homophobic corporate cultures and boards."

—John Brown former CEO, BP PLC

O ver the last decade, much progress has been made in shifting attitudes on sexual orientation.

Notwithstanding the progress made, even in enlightened organizations, homosexual and transgender workers are fearful of either coming out or being outed.

This is not surprising as companies in twenty-nine of the US states can still fire a worker for being gay. Also, according to the Human Rights Campaign, until late 2014 when Apple's CEO, Tim Cook came out, there was not a single openly gay CEO in the Fortune 1000 companies.

In 2007 BP PLC Chief John Brown resigned amid revelations he had lied in court on how he met his boyfriend. In a *Wall Street Journal* article on July 25, 2011, by Leslie Kwoh called "A Silence That Hangs Over CEO's" Brown stated, "Keeping executives from coming out are homophobic corporate cultures and Boards" and "companies are very conservative and the bigger the business is, the more conservative it is."

Similarly, in professional sports, very few athletes have had the courage to come out. Mark Tewksbury, the Canadian Olympic Gold Medallist in swimming, stated at the 2009 Vancouver Q Hall of Fame launch, "It's a difficult place to be if you are straight." "Sport is still a top down from policy makers," he told *Xtra*, Canada's GLBT magazine, adding, "it's very dogmatic and rule bound. People don't want to change rule structures. It's by nature, highly conservative. It's pretty much the last machinations of the old boys club."

Until Jason Collins, a veteran of 12 NBA seasons, announced in April of 2013 that he was gay there were no openly gay athletes in the NHL, NBA, and MLB. The NFL made history in May of 2014 when Michael Sam was chosen by St. Louis and became the first openly gay draft pick. In soccer Robbie Rodgers, the former member of the US National Team, revealed on his blog in February that he was gay. Had he announced earlier, he would have been the first openly gay male athlete to play in a major American team sport. Very few in broadcasting have come out, a rare exception being CNN's Anderson Cooper who did so in July 2012.

In entertainment, a 2012 survey by the actors union Equity revealed that only 57% of gay actors felt they could be open about their sexuality with their agent and one third had experienced homophobia in the workplace, saying it had come from other performers.

Case Study—No Way Out—Mark's Story

Mark worked for a midsized medical equipment company for twenty-two years. He started as an inventory control clerk working his way up and was recently promoted to head of purchasing. He joined the company after graduating from the local community college. The company is located in a midwestern city where Mark grew up. Mark and Lori married the year after he graduated college. Their two sons are now in their late teens.

In 2009 Mark was found dead in his car, which was parked in his garage, from carbon monoxide poisoning. Mark committed suicide.

While Mark's suicide came as a total shock to Lori and their sons, they knew there was something wrong for a long time, but did not know what. For two or so years prior Mark was not himself. He was withdrawn, irritable, depressed, lethargic, suffered stomach disorders, headaches and was restless at night, unable to sleep. He kept to himself and when asked what was going on would always answer, "Nothing really, just a bit of pressure at work," and told them that there was nothing to worry about.

Shortly after the funeral, John, a close friend of Mark's, asked to meet with Lori, indicating that he had some information that she should be aware of and would answer why Mark had taken his life. When they met, John was very distraught and said "If I had done something earlier, Mark would be alive today." John indicated to Lori that Mark asked him to tell Lori the whole story after "he left."

John told Lori that Mark approached him a month before he died to ask John for help, that he had no one else to turn to. Mark indicated to John that he had done something terrible and needed to make it right and he had to get out of the situation he had found himself in. Based on what Mark told him, John assumed that "getting out" meant that Mark was going to run away.

John started from the beginning. Mark's manager Ed was also a long service employee with the company. Mark and Ed had a reasonable working relationship but were not close socially outside of work. Ed was pretty rough around the edges and could be very crude when things upset him. Mark learned to live with it and rationalized Ed's behavior like everybody else did in the company by saying or thinking "Oh, that's just Ed."

In early 2006 Ed called Mark into his office and said, "I hear you are a f—ing faggot. Somebody told me that you are a regular at some queer joint called the Red Rooster." (The Red Rooster is a gay establishment in a neighbouring city.) Mark was flabbergasted and said, "I don't know what you are talking about, and even if I was, it is none of your business." Ed then pulled out three photos and said, "You're not only a f—ing faggot but you're a f—ing liar. You work for me and it is my f—ing business."

Mark was devastated. Not only did he risk losing his family should his sexuality become known, he feared for his own physical safety. Homosexuals in the Midwest have lost their lives. Only a decade earlier, Matthew Shepard, a young man from Wyoming, was beaten and left for dead hanging on a barbed wire fence after frequenting a gay bar.

This information from Ed floored Mark. He asked, "Who else knows?" Ed smiled and said "I always knew you were a pansy, so I decided to have you followed. The only other person is a private investigator who is paid to keep his mouth shut." Ed then proceeded to tell Mark that he had a little scheme in mind and if Mark wanted "Our little secret" kept that way, he would have to play along. Ed then ended the meeting by saying, "I will lay it out to you tomorrow." Thus began Mark's nightmare.

During his high school years Mark knew he was attracted to men. Mark resisted the temptations and felt that it was a passing phase. In grade twelve he started dating Lori, who was a year behind him. The city they lived in was small, fairly close knit and there were no opportunities for Mark to explore what he became to realise was not a passing phase. Mark was as closeted as one could be.

Ten or so years after Mark and Lori married, Mark attended a conference in Atlanta. It was there he met John who coincidentally was from the same city and alumnus of the college Mark had attended. Mark and John recognized each other and decided to have dinner. Over dinner they realized a mutual attraction and spent the remainder of the conference together. John was also married at the time and while not as closeted as Mark, he kept his sexuality a secret. Mark and John carried on an affair for less than two years and decided they should end it but remain close friends, which they were. John was the only person Mark could be "out" with and John introduced him to "the scene" in the neighbouring city.

After the confrontation with Ed, Mark was petrified. He had been so careful to protect his secret, now his worst fears were becoming reality. Mark was convinced that if he were exposed he would lose everything, Lori would leave him, his sons would disown him, it could kill his ailing parents, he would be shunned by the community and Ed would find a way to force him out of the company. All night he wondered what Ed had in mind to keep "our little secret" kept that way.

Early the next morning Ed was already in Mark's office waiting for Mark. "Let's go for a ride," Ed suggested. In Ed's car, Ed laid out the "scheme." "I will keep our little secret if you arrange for ten of our vendors to give us kickbacks. If you don't I will go to Jim (the CFO who was Ed's boss) and tell him that you approached me with the idea to keep me quiet, because you found out I knew you were a faggot." Mark had to have Ed stop the car. He quickly opened the door and threw up what little he had eaten for dinner the night before. What Ed was demanding went totally against Mark's value system. He prided himself on the relationships he had developed with the vendor community and now he was being blackmailed to betray the company he loved, the vendor community and himself.

"I can't do it," Mark declared.

"You don't have much of a choice, pansy boy; if you don't, you are going to be fired, and everyone will find out that you are a faggot who tried to keep it a secret by bribing me to do something illegal. Nobody will hire you again I'll see to it, you will be on the street." "Give me a couple of days to think about it," Mark asked. "Take your time, faggot," Ed responded.

Mark did not know what to do. He considered discussing it with Lori but he could not take the risk. The only person he could talk to about it was John, but what could John do other than lend a sympathetic ear. Mark seriously considered suicide at the time but decided that was a coward's way out.

Two days later Ed was waiting for Mark in his office. "Let's go for another ride," Ed suggested. This time they drove to the local gym that they both belonged to. They met in the dry sauna where they could be alone.

"Now here is how it works, I will give you the names of ten vendors who I know will co-operate. All you have to do is give them an amount to deposit each month in an offshore account and each month you will transfer the entire balance to another offshore account. I will give you instructions on how and where to open the account and the instructions on how to automatically have the balance in your account transferred to my account."

It started that week. Mark met with each vendor in a safe environment and they all agreed to the terms. Mark knew that this type of thing went on but had no idea, based on the reaction of the vendors, how it was almost expected. It was obvious to Mark that he was not the first person Ed recruited to engage in this type of activity. Mark always wondered how Ed could afford living in a multimillion dollar house, a stay-at-home wife, the expensive cars and exotic trips. Now he knew. He also wondered if the higher ups in the company questioned Ed's extravagant lifestyle.

The other thing that perplexed Mark was the lack of checks and balances in place to avoid this type of activity. All an auditor would have to do is a net/net price comparison and it would show that they were overpaying for many items.

For close to the next three years, Mark's life was a living hell. Not only was he engaged in this illegal activity, which, if he was caught, would land him in jail for a long time, but at every opportunity, when no one was within ear shot, Ed would call him a "f—ing faggot" or "pansy boy." Ed would also question Mark about his relationship with Lori and offer to "service her" as "obviously she is not getting it from you."

THE BULLY'S TRAP

During this period Ed became greedier and greedier. Periodically Ed would arrange for them to meet in the dry sauna at the gym, again to make sure no one could listen and make sure Mark was not wired. Even though Ed was a boorish goon, he was not stupid. At these meetings Ed would add to the vendor list and increase the amounts the others were paying. The total amount collected over this period exceeded seven million dollars.

From the beginning Mark kept a diary of every discussion he had with Ed and the vendors. He also had a record of each and every transaction. At some point he was going to expose Ed, the only problem is he did not know how.

Finally he figured it out. He would engage his friend, John. They met at John's house and Mark laid out the full story, giving John a copy of his diary and a record of all of the transactions. Mark indicated to John that "there was only one way to end this, I have to leave." John tried to convince Mark that he should go to the CEO of the company with this, to which Mark replied, "I just can't face him; this is my only way out."

Mark asked John to meet with Lori, "after I leave," and tell her the whole story. Mark indicated he wanted it to be Lori's decision on whether to go to the CEO of the company with the diary and the records.

A month later, Mark got out.

Lori quietly listened to the whole story. "Now it all makes sense," she commented. "I knew from the beginning that Mark was bisexual," she told John. "I also knew the two of you had a thing going, but I still loved him, we were best friends, had a wonderful relationship, and he was a great dad." Lori also indicated that being bi or gay was not a choice, the choice was whether to be out or not and Mark made his choice, which Lori respected because she knew that Mark believed if he came out it would hurt her and their sons.

141

Lori decided, after consulting with her sons, who wholeheart-edly concurred, that she and John needed to go to the CEO of the company and relay the full story.

The CEO readily agreed to meet with them. At the meeting he listened to the story, read the diary and reviewed the records of the transactions. After he was finished, he wept and said, "I don't know how Mark was able to bear this burden for as long as he did. Lori, I am so ashamed of what happened here and that Mark did not feel comfortable enough in coming to me with this.

"I would like to have a week to determine what to do," the CEO said, adding that he would like to meet with Lori and John again after the week. He also gave them an assurance that Mark's name and reputation would be protected in whatever action they decided to take.

That week the CEO met with the Chair of the Board of Directors and the Chair of Audit, gave them the full story and offered his resignation, which they indicated would not be necessary and they indicated that they too had to accept some responsibility for not having the checks and balances in place.

As promised the CEO met with Lori and John the following week to outline what the Board had decided.

A forensic audit was conducted that found that the kickbacks dated back to two years after Ed started with the company.

Ed was charged, convicted, sent to prison, and ordered to make full restitution.

All of the vendors involved avoided criminal charges by making full restitution and paying the company penalties for their actions.

The CFO's resignation was accepted. The CEO and the Board viewed him as being negligent.

Checks and balances were put in place and periodic audits are conducted to prevent this type of thing from happening in the future.

Lori will continue to receive Mark's compensation until he would have reached retirement age, after which she will receive his full pension benefits.

Mark and Lori's sons will receive full scholarships to a university of their choice from the company.

Mark's reputation was protected.

What People Go Through When They Fall Into The Bully's Trap

As I outlined in the Prologue, bullies are masters of deflection, who deceive and manipulate to achieve their end. Their intent is to break the target down to become what they want them to be, which in most cases is a problem employee, and/or the villain. When this happens, the target falls into a very calculated trap.

People who are targeted usually go through four stages:

1. Denial and Rationalization

2. Deterioration

3. Paying the Price

4. Closure

Stage 1—Denial and Rationalization

While people who are targeted realize that something is out of the norm, most do not identify it as being bullied. The initial reaction usually is to blame themselves by thinking, "I must have done something wrong" and believe that what they are experiencing will pass if they keep their head down. Also in most incidents they attribute the behavior of the bully to be a matter of style, versus a calculated plan to destroy them, even when the bullying persists over time. Another common rationalization is the assumption that bullying behavior is "that's just the way it is around here and to complain about it will be viewed as a sign of weakness". Rarely do people confide in others on what they have to endure again because they do not want to be viewed as weak and not able to cope.

It is at this stage where targets are vulnerable in becoming bullied bullies, particularly in those cultures that view bullies as heroes, and the bullying behaviors are a means to survive and advance.

Stage 2—Deterioration

As the bullying continues and the target continues to deal with it alone, it starts to affect the physical and emotional wellbeing of the target. They are under incredible stress, particularly if they feel that their job may be at risk. In the chapter called "Workplace Bullying and Post Traumatic Stress Disorder" you will see how people who become entrapped by persistent bullying suffer from Post Traumatic Stress Disorder (PTSD). An astounding 95 percent of targets suffer from PTSD.

At this stage the deterioration in performance and attitude becomes evident. This is all part of the bully's calculated plan. The target at this stage starts taking out his frustrations on others, both at work and at home, he withdraws from outside interests and in many instances starts to become dependent on alcohol or drugs to cope. The target is now fully in the bully's trap, and the bully has the ammunition needed to "appropriately deal with him."

Stage 3—Paying the Price

The bully armed with the ammunition will at this stage force the issue. The target is wounded, weak, alienated and alone. The bully wants the target gone and will try to get the target to quit or do something that allows him to fire for cause.

Stage 4—Closure

Being targeted is something that very few people can get closure on. They replay what has gone on over and over without being able to let it go. For some it leads to a total breakdown, and as you will see in the chapter called "Costs, Liabilities And Deadly Consequences" the only way they can get closure is suicide; and for others it is "going postal" and killing others.

For some, they seek closure through revenge. The following is a case study called "Seeking Revenge—Dean's Story" of an executive who was forced out by a bully. His revenge was helping employees become unionized, providing the competition with confidential information and discrediting the company with key clients, all of which resulted in the company going down. While I do not condone his actions, based on what I have experienced and what I have heard from others, it is completely understandable that a person would reach this breaking point.

Beyond the obvious costs and risks of bullying, the risk of losing reputation and brand value should be a major consideration for organizational leaders. Employees who are targeted may not seek revenge to the extent that is illustrated in the following case study, though the likelihood that they will speak badly of the organization is high.

Case Study—Seeking Revenge— Dean's Story

Dean was a Vice President of operations for a waste management company in Western Canada, a position that he held for just over nine years. In 2010 the company was sold to a multinational corporation and they appointed Mary as President and CEO. Mary had been with the multinational corporation for a number of years in their other companies.

From the outset, Mary made it clear to Dean that unless he significantly reduced operating costs, she would replace him. Dean felt that while there were opportunities to reduce costs, an investment in new equipment and technology would be required to reduce many of the manual processes. Previous owners had been reluctant to make the required investments and the company fell behind in benchmark comparisons to similar companies, including their competitors.

Mary's response to Dean was, "We are not going to invest another dime in this company—make do with what you have, force your people to work harder, and threaten them with outsourcing if they don't comply." Dean tried to reason with Mary, who said, "If you can't do it I will find someone who can."

Dean spent the next few months trying to improve the processes and looked for every avenue to reduce costs. Through his motivating skills he engaged employees to find ways to improve their productivity. Although this yielded results, they were not enough to satisfy Mary. For almost nine months Mary harassed Dean 24/7, she singled him out in meetings, berating him for putting the company at risk of closure because he was not getting costs cut fast enough, called him at home after hours, on weekends and holidays, demanding to know what he was doing.

The breaking point for Dean was a call he received from Mary on New Years Day of 2011, when Mary demanded that Dean fire ten percent of the workforce the next day. Dean told Mary that she was "crazy" and wanted to have an audience with Mary's boss. On the call Mary fired Dean for insubordination. After some persuading, Dean's request for a meeting with Mary's boss was granted, only to be told that Mary was a star performer who always came through with the numbers.

Dean wanted revenge. A month after he was fired he contacted a union official and worked undercover to recruit employees to join the union, which they did in record time. At the same time he went to the company's major competitors and gave them classified information, he also went to one of the major clients whose contract with the company was up for renewal and indicated that the company was at risk and they would be better advised to go to the major competitor, which they did. Six months after Dean was fired, the company declared bankruptcy.

Case Study—"The Target Becoming The Bully"—Janet's Story

In 2009 Janet, a registered nurse with over twenty years of service, transferred to a new hospital within her regional municipality.

While Janet knew most of the nursing staff at the hospital, she rarely socialized with them, wanting to separate her work from her personal life and avoid the political dynamics that existed in the other hospitals she worked in.

Although there were many aspects of nursing that Janet did not like, the joy of being able to ease the suffering of her patients negated the negatives.

Shortly after she joined, Janet observed a number of instances where Judy, one of her colleagues, verbally abused elderly patients and in some instances used undue physical force. Janet confronted Judy, who told her to mind her own business. The abuses by Judy continued and Janet confidentially lodged a complaint with the head nurse. The head nurse went to Judy and told her another nurse had lodged a complaint. Judy responded by indicating she knew it was Janet who squealed on her and told the head nurse that Janet was a trouble maker and a loner who did not get along with anyone.

For three months after lodging the complaint all of Janet's colleagues, including the head nurse, shunned her. The head nurse, who it turns out was a close friend of Judy's, started disciplining Janet for becoming too attached to the patients because she was doing things over and above what was required to make her patients comfortable. When Janet protested, the head nurse accused her of undermining her authority. When Janet went to human resources to complain, she was told nothing could be done and sided with the head nurse by indicating the extras that Janet gave to patients were not necessary and cost the hospital money.

Janet decided to take matters into her own hands and started gossiping to other nurses about Judy and the head nurse, relaying that Judy was abusing patients and the head nurse was condoning it because Judy and the head nurse were lesbians. Janet was disciplined by the hospital and the College of Nurses for this and almost lost her license to practice because of her actions. Janet became a bully who is targeted by another bully and she, not her tormentors, paid the price.

What Motivates Bullying

A s you have seen in Part One, most organizations allow, condone, encourage, and even expect their managers to bully. My research and that of others shows that the main reason people are targeted is to force them out.

The usual motivations and intentions are:

- To reduce labor costs

- Retaliation to punish the target

- Bigotry

- Exploitation—to get people to work harder and faster (it is the only way weak managers know how to manage)

- To exercise (abuse) their power

- To eliminate a threat

Reduce Labor Costs

Almost every day we hear in the media about questionable business practices. One area that needs to be exposed is organizations using bullying tactics to reduce employment costs. Older workers and long-term employees are particularly vulnerable. The formula is very simple; force senior employees out and replace them with younger ones at a lower pay rate, thereby reducing the overall average salary. If people quit, severance is avoided. By doing this there is an added benefit for those companies who have a defined benefit plan: their pension costs and unfunded liability is greatly reduced. While I do not want to debate the false economics of this, I only want to expose it for what it is, ethically and morally dishonest and wrong.

Precedence on this could be based on the outcome of two class action suits that Federal Express has faced. The two suits claim that Fed Ex has actual policies and practices in place that are designed to push employees out before they reach age fifty-five. The plaintiffs in the case allege that Fed Ex discriminates against couriers over forty years old, especially if they have over ten years' seniority, by taking away their routes and setting unrealistic performance targets, and that the company gave supervisors lists of older workers to target for increased supervision, discipline, and harassment.

Studies have found that for over 70 percent of the bullying targets, the only way they could stop the bullying was to leave their employment.

Retaliation

While many employers claim to have an open door policy and tools in place such as a whistleblower hot line, not all welcome contrary viewpoints and reports of irregularities or wrongdoing. Some shoot the messenger and retaliate against employees who don't follow the party line, who fight an injustice, or who report irregularities or wrong doing.

My experience with companies who have whistleblower hot lines is that executives and boards are proud of how few calls are made to the hotline without even considering that employees and vendors may not trust the system.

In 2009, retaliation moved up to tie with race discrimination as the most common type of charge filed with the U.S. Equal Employment Opportunity Commission (EEOC).

Even in the United States, which lags behind all westernized jurisdictions on anti-bullying legislation, the Supreme Court has issued a declaration that changes the grounds on which retaliation claims are actionable. With the Burlington Northern vs. White decision of the U.S. Supreme Court (2006) the increased action is likely to keep growing. By making this decision the court has effectively broadened the standard to be allowed in unlawful retaliation claims made against employers so that courts will now apply a different standard for analyzing adverse employment action in retaliation cases than discrimination cases.

The demise of organizations and the global meltdown could have been avoided had people in the know reported the wrong doing—they did not, largely for fear of being retaliated against. In most cases the whistleblowers are viewed as traitors and subject to bullying as punishment for their crime.

According to over ten thousand cases from the UK and National Work Advice Line in cases reported through its website, the fifth reason for being bullied is "blowing the whistle on malpractice fraud, illegal legalities, breaches of rules, regulations and procedures, or raising health and safety issues."

Bigotry

Despite the millions that organizations spend on diversity and sensitivity training, bigotry and hatred still is very evident.

Race discrimination ties retaliation as the most common type of charge filed with the U.S. Equal Opportunity Commission.

International Communications Research conducted a phone survey of 623 randomly selected employed Americans in February of 2006 and here were some of the findings:

- "30 percent overheard racial slurs
- 20 percent reported ridicule of perceived or legitimate sexual orientation
- 20 percent experienced age bias
- 35 percent of men and 28 percent of women overheard abuses from the highest level."

Exploitation and Weak Management

"All cruelty springs from weakness"

—Seneca

Where there is ambiguity and subjectivity in an organization's performance management process, there are opportunities for bullying.

A host of European studies found that many of the environmental characteristics that contribute to bullying are actually describing the functional features of a work unit, and most of them are also factors related to leadership style and supervisory practices. Heinz Leymann commented in his article, "The Content and Development of Mobbing at Work," that of the 800 case studies where mobbing (UK term for bullying) occurred frequently, an almost stereotypical pattern of poorly organized working methods and weak management were found.

Research suggests that overloaded and bullied employees tend to work for organizations that are declining or shrinking, where the management style is bureaucratic and reactive.

When people fall into the bully's trap, they become as the character Vera in Vera's story, a poor performer with an attendance problem and bad attitude. This gives the bully the ammunition to take disciplinary action up to and including discharge. This is a huge catch twenty-two for the target and a huge enabler for the bully. Kaj Bjorkqvist, Karin Osterman, and Monika Hjelt-Back in "Aggression Among University Employees" wrote: "Like domestic violence, it can be difficult for people to talk about workplace bullying."

This has made it difficult to capture the true dimensions of the problem, and helps explain why it is not always recognized. Like any abusive relationship, people tend to deny or minimize abuse as a way to survive it. The workplace provides a further wrinkle in that bullying behavior can be easily concealed by or disguised as "strong management." Likewise, it is difficult for targets to report, as targets risk retribution and job loss. It can also have a stigmatizing effect, since to admit to being harassed at work is something others might see as a weakness or an inability to cope.

Abuse of Power

"Power over a man's subsistence
amounts to power over his will."

—Alexander Hamilton

People who have power and have to rely on their position to get others to do things or not do things are bullies, and this is abuse of power, particularly if people are forced into doing things that are unethical or in conflict with their values and beliefs.

In the media, reports of corruption by executives and politicians have become commonplace. What is common in most of the stories we hear about is how long the corruption has gone on without people in the know coming forward. There is little question that these people were bullied into silence.

In organizations where there are no checks and balances, bullies can and do target employees purely to assert their power. Again, 70 percent of bullying is boss to subordinate—and the boss has the power of position and is in a position to use power to instill fear.

Although it is common for coworkers to bully their colleagues, it is more often top down. When it starts at the top it does impact the entire organizational culture.

Eliminating a Threat

Many bullies are insecure despite their confident facade. When bullies feel their power or status is threatened by a coworker or subordinate they will not hesitate in targeting them.

During my career, I have been involved in a number of reorganizations. As reorganizations usually involve massive change—they also usually trigger reactions from those who fear losing power and control.

Case Study—They Wanted To Push Me Out—William's Story

In 2007 William quit his job as a driver for a major transportation and logistics company after twelve years of employment. At the time William was forty-three years old. William thought that he would have no problem finding another job; however, with the economic downturn and the unemployment rate in southern California reaching double digits, this was not the case. At the time of writing this book, William was still out of work. Recently he and his family moved in with his in-laws as the house that they had lived in for eight years went into foreclosure. There is a bit of income coming in from William's wife, who works part-time for a National Drug Chain. There is some hope that William may be able to get his job back and be paid for the period he has been off as his union has filed a grievance on his behalf and for a number of others who either quit or were fired.

Until 2006 William thought that he would be a lifer with the company. The company provided good wages and benefits and had a defined pension plan. Working conditions were excellent and the vehicles were always clean and in good working order. The company prided itself on their employee relations and wanted to be known as "an employer of choice." They had a huge Human Resources Department and all of the "state of the art" employment policies, procedures and practices. The majority of employees were represented by a union.

In 2006 the company negotiated a new collective agreement with the union. The main changes were a two-tier wage and benefit structure, and a change in the pension plan from a defined benefit to a defined contribution. Existing employees maintained their wage grid and benefit coverage and had the option of switching their pension to the defined contribution plan. New hires, after the agreement was ratified, would go on the new grid and the much reduced benefit plan and the defined contribution pension plan.

Almost immediately after the new collective agreement went into effect there was a major restructuring at the supervisory level and Geoff, a twenty eight year old with an accounting background became William's boss. William's former boss, who was in his mid fifties, not yet eligible for early retirement was laid off. It turns out that most mid level supervisory, managerial administrative and professional employees who were over age forty with ten or more years service got caught up in the restructuring.

A few years earlier, the company had installed a very sophisticated truck routing system which made the loads and multiple deliveries efficient. The system featured an engineered labor standards (a system to measure productivity), that is the time it would take to make all of the deliveries. The system was very flexible in that it factored in traffic patterns at various times of the day and week. The system also allowed the company to give customers a fairly tight window of time when to expect to receive their deliveries. Until William started working for Geoff, with few exceptions he met or exceeded the standards as set out by the system. The few exceptions were when traffic was unusually heavy or there were delays due to road closures. William and his coworkers felt the system was fair and it also allowed them to earn bonuses for meeting and exceeding the standards.

A few weeks after Geoff started, he met with William to get to know him. Geoff asked William to go over his routine, which William did. "It's pretty basic really, I clock in, go to the dispatch office to get my schedule of deliveries, do a circle check of the truck for safety compliance, scan the bar code of each item to make sure that everything is accounted for and then I am on my way." Geoff asked how long this all took, to which William replied that he could usually be on the road within half hour.

"Isn't that a bit long?" asked Geoff to which William said, "The system doesn't think so." Geoff said, "It is my understanding that the system is a guideline, and I think you should be able to cut it in half." William indicated he would try to see if he could do it quicker.

Geoff checked every day for the next two weeks, and while William shaved off a few minutes it still averaged out to the half hour. Geoff met with William after the two weeks and said, "You are not trying very hard, are you," to which William replied, "I'm doing the best I can." Geoff became very agitated and indicated that he was going to keep a close eye on William and that he felt William was not measuring up to other drivers, who exceeded the standards more often than he did.

After this confrontation William started having real difficulty in meeting the standards, at least three times per week for the next four weeks he ran over his schedule, and the deliveries went beyond the tight window to the customer.

Every time this would happen Geoff would berate William, often in front of the dispatcher and other drivers. After four weeks, William went to John, his union representative, and indicated what was happening. John said, "William, if you are not meeting standards, they have the right to go after you."

The following week William was called in to a meeting with Geoff, John and a human resource person. William was given a written warning to improve his performance and unless his performance improved he could face further disciplinary action up to and including discharge.

Over the next number of weeks William pushed as hard as he could, took as many shortcuts as he could, stopped doing the circle check of his truck, went over the speed limits, and hurried through each delivery. There was no time for any small talk with the customers and yet while there was improvement, there were still an unacceptable number of times he was not able to meet the standards.

During this time he noted that a number of other drivers were having the same difficulties; in fact, four had recently been fired for poor performance. William and some of his coworkers started to compare notes and discovered that all of the new hires had no trouble meeting the standards and most of the senior drivers were not. One of the senior drivers asked, "Do you think they are overriding the system?" The thought had occurred to William (drivers have a lot of time to think), and he decided to meet with John again to lay out this possibility.

John indicated that he would request that the union's staff Industrial Engineer do an audit of the system. This occurred a week later and the Industrial Engineer validated that the system was fair and that it did not appear that it was being tampered with.

Over the next three months William was continually berated by Geoff and two more disciplinary meetings were held. At the second meeting Geoff indicated that unless there was significant improvement in the next two weeks, he would have no choice but to fire William. During this time frame six more senior drivers left, some were fired, others quit.

There was no significant improvement. John called William and advised him to resign and if he did not he would be fired and the union would not be able to protect him. He also pointed out that William would have far more difficulty in finding another job if he was fired. William submitted his resignation the next day giving two weeks' notice. Geoff accepted William's resignation and told him he would be paid for the two weeks but he did not have to come in.

All of this was not making sense to John and he kept wondering why none of the new hires were having difficulty and almost all of the senior drivers were. John then checked with the Industrial Engineer to make sure the system had integrity. The Industrial Engineer took great offence and said, "I told you it was; who are you to be questioning my professional ability?" John thought the response was a bit extreme, all he was doing was checking to be sure.

A few weeks later at a quarterly meeting held by the union, John relayed what was happening to the senior drivers at his location. Every other union representative John spoke to indicated the exact same thing was happening at their locations. "Remember after the last set of negotiations the company had a restructuring and they laid off people who had a lot of service?" one of the union representatives asked, adding, "Do you think that they are doing the same thing to the drivers?" Then it registered with John, thinking that with the two tier compensation structure it was certainly an incentive for the company to get rid of more senior people, and if they got them to quit it was like winning a trifecta at a horse race; they avoided paying severance, reduced their average hourly rate and reduced their unfunded pension liability.

John, with the help of union representatives at a number of other locations, compiled a list of people who quit or were fired since the new agreement went into effect. They found that there was indeed a pattern. Ninety percent were over age forty with over ten years service. One of the representatives suggested to John that he approach one of the new supervisors brought in by the company who left shortly after joining. John was able to connect with him.

Fred was a twenty-six-year-old who after leaving the company worked for an automotive supply firm. Like Geoff, Fred had an accounting background. Fred initially was reluctant to speak with John, as when he left the company they insisted that he sign a confidentiality agreement and a breach of this could leave him open to a law suit. The head of Human Resources who conducted Fred's exit interview also implied that if Fred was to expose the company in any way he would be blacklisted for years. Although Fred was concerned about speaking to John, his conscience dictated that the story had to come out, too many people were having their lives' destroyed and it needed to be stopped. John and Fred met at a safe location and Fred relayed his experience.

Fred's first assignment was to learn the truck routing and standards system and then how to override the system. After three weeks of intensive one-on-one training he was assigned to a location and became a supervisor. Two weeks later his manager gave Fred a list of sixteen drivers that, in the manager's words, "were troublemakers and needed to be forced out of the company." The manager indicated that Fred's number one priority was to get them out. There was also a financial incentive involved: for every driver on the list who quit, Fred would receive a bonus of six thousand dollars, and for every driver who was fired, three thousand, five hundred dollars. The reason for the difference is if the driver was fired, there would likely be severance involved.

The method to force the drivers out was to go into the system and alter the standard to the point where the targets would be impossible to achieve. The important thing was to phase this in for each driver on the target list so it would not be obvious. Once a trend of "not meeting standards" was established, Fred was to go after the driver and harass them to the point they quit. The manager indicated that the union's staff Industrial Engineer could do an audit of the system but not to worry as, "he is in our hip pocket."

Initially Fred played along, but soon he realized that the drivers on the list were not the trouble makers the manager described but decent hard workers who were targeted in a systemic way so that the company could significantly reduce their labor costs. This was totally contrary to Fred's value system and he resigned.

Fred insisted on an exit interview with the Head of Human Resources and relayed the story to her. As indicated earlier Fred was warned to keep quiet.

John prepared a report and met with the President of the union. The staff Industrial Engineer was confronted and confessed that he was paid off by management to validate the integrity of the system. In exchange for a signed and witnessed affidavit he was allowed to resign, which protected his retirement benefits.

A grievance was filed on behalf of every driver targeted who either quit or was fired subsequent to the new collective agreement. The union is also in discussions with other employee groups who were similarly targeted to convince them to file a class action suit against the company. (As these groups were not represented by the union, they were unable to file a grievance.)

Predictably the company is denying any wrongdoing and vigorously fighting the grievance filed.

Case Study—Exploitation—Leila's Story

Leila never wanted to leave the Philippines. Married with two small children, she and her husband struggled financially to make ends meet. Leila, a nurse by training, and her husband, a construction worker, found themselves in and out of the workforce due to the country's high rate of unemployment and poverty. When they were both working, they barely made enough money to pay the rent on a small one-bedroom apartment in Manila, let alone buy a house where the family could reside and raise their children properly.

Leila had a sister working as a nanny in Canada. When Leila found herself out of work for nearly six months, and her husband lost his job, she decided to apply to work abroad as well. It was a tough decision, for she knew she would be leaving her two small children, ages four and two. But she promised to write every day and return for visits every year. Leila knew from her sister and friends working in Canada that she could earn as much as $1,200 a month, three times as much as she earned in the Philippines. She would send all of her salary home to support her husband. Leila also discovered, during a training course to work as a caregiver in Canada, that after two years of employment, she could apply for

Canadian permanent residency, essentially citizenship. She began to dream of offering her own children better lives and access to good Western schools and universities. She also dreamed of becoming a nurse in Canada when she completed the Live-in Caregiver Program (LCP). The LCP states that a nanny must complete two years of full-time employment within a three-year period. While in the LCP the caregiver must live in her employer's home.

It took six months for Leila to complete a required training program in Manila, which taught her basic care giving skills that she already knew from nursing. She then paid an employment agency the equivalent of $2000, which she borrowed from a bank, to find her a placement in Canada. Finally, her employer, a wealthy woman in Vancouver, British Columbia, agreed to sponsor Leila under the LCP to work as her nanny. The woman, Rita, had five children, ranging in age from four to sixteen. Leila would be responsible, or so the letter of employment stated, for looking after the children only.

Leila said her painful goodbyes and left for Canada. She arrived in Vancouver on an unusually snowy day in January. From the get go, Leila encountered one problem after another. Her employer didn't pick her up at the airport for nearly three hours. Leila waited in the terminal, impatiently pacing back and forth. The telephone number given to her by her employment agency didn't work. Leila had no way of reaching her new boss. When her new employer did arrive, she said she had to run some errands before taking Leila to the house. Leila, who was tired due to both the long flight and the time difference, was put to work right away, preparing a dinner for the entire family and cleaning up before she was able to even unpack.

Her days unfolded much the same. Leila was told she had to be up and working by 6 a.m., preparing breakfasts and lunches for the children for school. The youngest, age 4, only attended kindergarten half a day, so Leila was responsible for caring for him in the mornings. After she walked the older children to school, she had to clean the dishes, do laundry, vacuum and clean the washrooms, all the while looking after the 4-year-old. None of the children did chores and were not neat. Leila found herself cleaning up their rooms. She then had to make two dinners: one for the children and another for her employers, who ate later. Often she was not finished cleaning the dinner dishes and kitchen until nine or ten at night. Her employers also had dinner parties every week, at which Leila was told she had to cook and serve. Leila found herself working seven days a week, from about 6:00 a.m. until 9:00 p.m.

If this wasn't bad enough, Leila then learned that her employer was docking room and board from her salary. Leila would only be earning $600 a month. Leila's bedroom was a cot set up in the basement beside the furnace. She prayed to the whirl of the machine, and in the damp winter months shivered under her blankets. There was no door to her room, so the children could come and go as they pleased. Leila was also not allowed to use the computer to email or call her family accept for Sunday mornings and only for one hour.

All the while, her female employer said she was one of the family and should make herself feel comfortable. But she wasn't allowed to eat with the family. She had to eat on her own and she was not allowed to buy her own food. She knew no one except a few nannies she began meeting at the park when she took the four-year-old. She felt lonely and isolated. One day, some of the Filipino nannies Leila was befriending at the park told her to speak to her employer about having one day off a week, if not two, and to reduce her hours so she could have evenings free to pray and knit, as she liked to make her children sweaters. Leila got the courage to do so. Her employer was furious, wanting to know with whom she was speaking who would advise her so poorly. Her employer took her passport and said that if she didn't do as she was told, Leila could return to the Philippines. She would put her back on the airplane but there was no way she was staying in Canada unless she followed her rules. "I will have you deported!" she screamed at Leila.

Leila was heartbroken. When she finally had a chance to call her husband, she broke down crying. But she couldn't tell him the truth as to why. She was homesick and feeling like she had made a big mistake. She told her husband, instead, that she just missed their children, but the job was going well. She didn't want him to worry about her.

Leila's employer gave her more work to do than ever. Her employer would make lists of things she had to do during the day, including cleaning the silver ware, dropping clothes off at the dry cleaner, cleaning the fridge and doing the gardening. The family also had two dogs that Leila was now responsible for walking.

Then one day, Leila was in the kitchen and the four-year-old called her "yellow skin." Leila was trying to get him to eat some carrots. He threw them at Leila's face and hissed: "You're not my mom. You can't tell me what to do. Go home, yellow skin." Leila got angry with the boy and said that carrots were good for him to eat and that he should not call people names. The boy started wailing, alerting the attention of Leila's employer, who came running. When she saw the child upset, she got mad at Leila. When Leila recounted what the child had said to her, her employer slapped her across the face. "How dare you accuse my son of being bad! Go to your room."

Leila's employer started docking her salary whenever anything on her list was not completed. Leila felt shy and insecure around all the children. She walked with her head down and kept her gaze to the floor. The once happy and upbeat young woman fell into a deep depression. She feared for her physical safety as her employer had her passport. She was overworked and tired.

The other nannies at the park recognized that Leila was being bullied and through several meetings got her to open up about the emotional blackmail going on at the home. The training programs in the Philippines did not tell Leila she had legal rights in Canada, even under the Live-In Caregiver Program, including a locked room to sleep in, overtime pay and days off. Leila feared coming forward filing a complaint with immigration because her employer had her passport and said she would have her deported should she disobey any order. The nannies said this was also against the law. Leila, nonetheless, was too afraid to do anything. All she could think about was the better life she was giving her children through her salary and their eventual residency in Canada.

But things in the home turned worse. One night, her male employer came into the furnace room drunk and tried to attack Leila. She fended him off by throwing her Bible at him. He was too drunk to protest and just passed out. The next day, however, her female employer fired her, saying that she had come on to her husband and that she was a slut. Leila had an hour to pack her things and find somewhere to go. On the way out the door, her employer returned the passport.

Luckily, Leila had the other nannies, and they referred her to an agency in Vancouver who helps live-in caregivers in distress. Leila eventually found another job with a good employer who pays her fairly, does not overwork her and does not threaten her with deportation. Leila discovered that most nannies in Canada are from the Philippines and that few know they have legal and human rights. Even if they do know, most are too afraid while under the program to file complaints against their employers. The LCP is ripe with abuse: from physical harassment to emotional blackmail. Many have called it modern-day slavery, in which the workplace has moved from the business towers to the kitchens and living rooms, and many parents seem to take advantage of the power they have over these women from developing countries, desperate to earn incomes to support their families and provide better lives for their children. Leila was a broken woman after her first experience in Canada, and her story represents so many others.

Bullying and Stakeholders External To The Organization

S takeholders other than employees are not immune from being bullied.

There are numerous reported incidents:

- In policing, brutality seems routine (the LAPD and RCMP being the most notorious).

- In nursing, patients being abused by healthcare providers and healthcare providers being bullied by patients and or the patient's family members.

- In education, teachers and professors seeking sexual favours in exchange for higher marks, and students and or parents bullying teachers in retaliation for not progressing or receiving lower marks.

- In retail and the service industry, customers bullying sales people.

As with employees, it is difficult to capture the true dimensions of the problem because the targets and bystanders are afraid to report. In policing, the use of cameras to record interactions between officers and citizens they apprehend is proving to be an effective deterrent.

⟨∽⟩

In Dictatorial and Disjointed cultures, particularly if there are no appropriate checks and balances, Service Providers and Vendors are subject to bullying, usually under the rationalization that the buyer is just driving a hard bargain and is a tough negotiator and considered a hero. In organizations that have lax ethical standards, bully buyers prosper.

Case Study—Learning From the Parents—Toni's Story

Until June of 2009 Toni was a teacher at a Private School for girls. Toni was regarded as an exceptionally good teacher and received high scoring in her performance reviews and feedback from students in each of the five years she taught there. Prior to her posting at this school Toni spent eleven years in the public school system. Toni also has a Master of Education degree.

In January of 2009 the parents of one of Toni's seventh grade students asked to meet with her. At the meeting the parents expressed their displeasure at how their daughter Julie was being graded. Toni indicated to the parents that while Julie definitely had the potential for higher grades, her attitude and not applying herself were holding her back. Julie's parents reacted badly to this and indicated that they would take the matter up with Margaret, the school's head.

The next day Toni was called into Margaret's office. Margaret indicated that Julie's parents had lodged a complaint against her. The complaint was that Toni was unfair in the grading she gave Julie. They also indicated that Toni was very rude to them when they met. Toni gave Margaret her side of the story and indicated that she was very fair in the grades she gave, in that there was very little subjectivity. Margaret asked Toni to reassess, to which Toni responded that she would be happy to, conditional on Julie being retested in the subjects that she had scored low in. Margaret felt that this would be appropriate and advised the parents, who did not like the idea but agreed provided that Julie be given three weeks to study for the exams. Toni made the observation that giving Julie this kind of time to study for the retesting could have her falling behind in her current courses.

Three weeks later Julie took the exams and the grading was marginally better, also as Toni predicted Julie was falling behind in her current courses. The parents went back to Margaret and complained that Julie was set up for failure and Toni had made the re-examination tougher than the original tests. They also complained that Toni was retaliating against Julie by being harder on her than other students and that this was the reason Julie was falling further behind. Margaret supported Toni by indicating that Toni had warned them that Julie's falling behind could occur because her focus would be on the retesting at the expense of her current courses. She also indicated that in the five years Toni had taught there, no complaints of this nature had ever been lodged.

For the next few weeks Margaret received at least one call a week from Julie's parents with complaints ranging from how Toni was treating Julie, ignoring her, to singling her out with the most difficult questions, making fun of her in front of other students and threatening to give her failing grades. Margaret went to Toni each and every time a complaint was made. Toni denied every allegation and asked Margaret to investigate by interviewing Julie and other students in the class. Margaret did this and found Julie to be very belligerent. In speaking to other students when asked, "Does Ms. Allen single any students out for special treatment or punishment?" every one indicated that they felt that Toni treated everyone the same and made a point of telling Margaret how much they liked Toni. One of the students mentioned that Julie had told her "my parents are going to get Ms. Allen fired."

This validated for Margaret that Julie's parents were definitely out to get Toni. Margaret met with Richard, the long-standing

Chair of the Board, about her concerns and asked him to intervene with Julie's parents. Richard indicated that he was uncomfortable doing this as the parents had already approached him on this and he felt that there was some merit to the concerns they had about Toni. Margaret was dumbfounded and asked why he had not come to her. Richard responded by indicating he had questions regarding how she (Margaret) handled the situation and wanted to consult with other Board members before he approached her. "Well I expect that you will do this before the week is finished, because if you don't I will call a meeting with the entire Board so that I can relay to them what is going on. You are obviously taking Julie's and her parents' word on this over mine and I do not have the confidence that you will properly represent and support Toni and myself on this matter."

Richard did not expect this response and tried to backtrack by indicating that he had not formed a judgment but wanted advice from others before he proceeded further. "Well I don't understand why you did not come to me first," Margaret responded, adding, "We have a situation where Toni is being bullied by Julie and her parents and I want it stopped; that's why I came to you." Richard and Margaret agreed to meet early the next week to determine a course of action.

The following Monday, Richard and Margaret met, and Richard started by telling Margaret that Julie's family had a long history with the school and the parents were major donors. "I am well aware of this and I do not understand why that should have any bearing on the situation; it does not give them the license to bully," Margaret interjected. "Well the Board does not share your view; in fact they agree with Julie's parents that Toni is the bully here," Richard replied.

Richard added that the Board had decided that Toni should be let go and directed Margaret to inform her. Margaret indicated that she disagreed with this decision, and if the Board did not reconsider she would view this as a lack of confidence in her and would view this as constructive dismissal. Richard then informed

Margaret that he considered this insubordination and fired her. Margaret went to Toni to indicate what was coming down.

Toni thanked Margaret for standing up for her and was distressed that Margaret lost her position because of it. Margaret told Toni that it would have been impossible for her to stay. Both Margaret and Toni filed constructive dismissal suits and settled out of court for considerably more than they would have received under normal severance arrangements because the Board did not want to have this made public.

A new Head was recruited. Julie's new teacher was forced to fudge her grades. Richard and the Board are still in place.

Case Study—The Customer Is Always Right—Allen's Story

Allen was a Sales Associate in the Women's Department of a high-end department store chain. He joined them in January of 2010 after moving back to Toronto from New York City, where he spent eleven years with a similar high-end retailer.

In May of 2010 a customer, Ms. Jones, bought an evening gown from Allen. While Ms. Jones was on the customer data base as a frequent shopper, this was the first time Allen sold to her. After the sale, Nancy, another sales associate went to Allen and said, "I'll bet you a drink that she returns the dress on Monday." Allen asked, "Why do you say that?" "Oh, she does it all the time, here and at other stores. When she has a fancy function to go to she 'buys' a garment, wears it to the event and returns it after, claiming either it is flawed, bad fit or she didn't like it after she got home." Allen asked Nancy, "Why is she not flagged in the system?" Nancy indicated that the rumour has it that Ms. Jones is well connected in the community and if there is any trouble she has the ability to convince other customers to boycott the store.

Sure enough, the following Monday Ms. Jones returned the gown, claiming that the color just was not right for her. Allen indicated that he had to check with the Manager. Nigel, the manager, was very familiar with Ms. Jones and gave the approval for a credit. When Allen objected, Nigel said, "Don't fight it, kid, that's the way it is," adding, "Remember one thing Allen, around here the customer is always right."

In giving Ms. Jones the credit Allen asked her how she enjoyed the event on Saturday night. In a haughty tone Ms. Jones asked, "What are you implying, young man?" "Nothing really, my friends saw you there."

The next morning Allen was called into Nigel's office and told that Ms. Jones had called the owner of the store to complain that Allen had been impertinent. Allen told Nigel what he had said and observed that Ms. Jones obviously made the connection that he knew that she had worn the returned gown to the event. Nigel told Allen that the owner wanted Allen to send a note of apology with a one hundred dollar gift certificate (which would be deducted from his commission). Allen refused and was fired. Nigel did not like what he had to do and said, "I am sorry, Allen, it is out of my hands and the owner is insistent."

Allen filed for wrongful dismissal and the case proceeded to discovery. Allen did his homework and found ten instances where Ms. Jones had made purchases of evening gowns over a two-year period and made returns after she had worn them at events. He also had pictures that were in the society pages of the major newspaper, including the gown he had "sold" to her.

Allen's lawyer indicated to the store's lawyer that they intended on calling Ms. Jones as a witness. When the owner became aware of this she instructed the lawyer to do whatever it took to settle. Allen received a handsome cash settlement and letters of apology from the owner and Ms. Jones (something that Allen insisted be part of the settlement).

How Big is the Issue?

In the interviews conducted with organizational leaders ("Altering the Attitudes of Organizational Leaders"), most felt bullying in the workplace was no big deal. This view is not shared by the workers. Anecdotal evidence suggests that almost everyone (including the leaders interviewed) has in some way been impacted over the course of their careers.

In December of 2011 *The Windsor Star* in Toronto, Ontario, reported that forty percent of Canadians are bullied at work. They cited Jacqueline Power, Assistant Professor of Management at the Odette School of Business, who has done extensive research on bullying in the workplace. According to Power, bullying is virtually never reported to management because when people do report, "they don't get much support and human resource managers don't often respond to the allegations."

European research into the problem began in the early 1980s in Scandinavian countries and spread during the late 1990s to other European countries, Australia, New Zealand, and Asia.

It was through the work of Loraleigh Keaschly (Wayne State University, Detroit, MI) in the 1990s that a conceptual framework for workplace bullying emerged in the United States. Prior to this there has been very little research in English on the topic.

According to the UK's *The Daily Telegraph*, a 2010 UK online poll of ten thousand people found that 92 percent believe they are the target of workplace taunts and intimidation, with 56 percent believing it is a serious problem in their office, shop or factory. It is also found that just under 50 percent blame their immediate manager for bullying them, while a similar proportion claimed their complaints were not properly dealt with.

Another UK study found that 53 percent had been bullied at work and 78 percent witnessed bullying at work.

The 2010 UK poll indicated that 51 percent of the British workforce are on the hunt for a new job, and the top reason is a "feud" with a boss or coworker, according to 53 percent of the 2,000 respondents.

Based on the research done to date it is reasonable to believe that the majority of employees, at some time during their career, will be exposed to systematic bullying or other forms of abusive behavior either directly or indirectly.

Costs, Liabilities And Deadly Consequences

"Workplace bullying—in any form—is bad for business.
It destroys teamwork, commitment and morale."

—Tony Morgan, Chief Executive, The Industrial Society

In *The Cost Of Bad Behavior: How Incivility is Damaging Your Business and What To Do About It,* Christine Porath, Ph.D., from the University of Southern California indicated that time wasted at work or spent searching for another job could cost companies up to $300 billion a year. Further, the American Institute of Stress (AIS) estimates that one million workers are absent each workday in the USA due to stress. The Institute calculated that it costs companies $300 billion a year in absenteeism, health expenses, and programs to help workers manage stress. This estimate does not include the cost of reduced productivity due to lowered morale, recruitment and training costs for new hires, stress related workman's comp claims, bad press, or litigation.

In a poll of 800 managers and employees in seventeen industries Christine Porath and her associate Christine Pearson found: "Among workers who've been on the receiving end of incivility:

- 48 percent intentionally decreased their work effort.

- 47 percent intentionally decreased the time spent at work.

- 38 percent intentionally decreased the quality of their work.

- 80 percent lost work time worrying about the incident.

- 63 percent lost work time avoiding the offender.

- 66 percent said that their performance declined.

- 78 percent said that their commitment to the organization declined.

- 12 percent said that they left their job because of the uncivil treatment.

- 25 percent admitted to taking their frustrations out on customers."

Although difficult to calculate, brand and reputation value takes a major hit in instances where violence in the workplace is exposed in the media. Consider what Rutgers University is experiencing after the video exposing bullying exploded in the media.

And the costs are more than just financial.

In the United States, an average of fifteen to twenty people are murdered weekly while at work. According to the U.S. National Institute for Occupational Safety and Health, homicide in the workplace is the fastest growing form of murder. Homicide is the leading cause of on-the-job death for women and the second leading cause for men. A further one million people are physically assaulted in the workplace every year, and even more are subjected to verbal violence. According to the US Dept. of Justice, BJS, 7/28/98, the workplace is the most dangerous place to be in America. The problem is so pervasive that the Center for Disease Control has classified workplace violence as a national epidemic.

An example is Christopher Dorner, the former LAPD officer who is alleged to have killed four people and targeted as many as fifty other officers and their families in revenge for his 2008 firing. His act of terrorism ended in a barrage of bullets and a blazing fire in a cabin in California's San Bernadino Mountains on February 12, 2013. There is now an investigation in response to suggestions that Dormer was bullied by officers he targeted and blamed for his being fired.

In South Korea after a series of events, one involving a bullied marine corporal who went on a shooting rampage killing four marines and wounding another, and a number of suicides, where bullying was a factor, a military culture of bullying and beating is drawing scrutiny by the Government of Korea's Defense Ministry.

In September of 2009 Jim Badasci, who worked at Fresno Equipment in Fresno, California, for ten years, went to work with a shot gun and killed a fellow coworker. Four others convinced him to stop shooting, and rather than killing them Badasci killed himself. A fellow coworker indicated what Badasci did was out of character and told Mark Ames of "The Exiled" that Badasci had "been driven to desperation by a particular supervisor and the company's tolerance of the supervisor's mistreatment."

A documentary, *Murder By Proxy—How America Went Postal* gives a dramatic history of the increasing number of mass murders in the United States and how bullying in the workplace is a major factor.

A United Nations report in 1996 estimated that worldwide, between 500,000 and 1.2 million people commit suicide every year (UN 1996). Real suicide rates are estimated to be 50-60 percent higher due to the stigma associated with reporting the deaths as such. Death by suicide exceeds the death toll of traffic accidents. While there is very little research to date on specific links of suicides or attempted suicides due to workplace bullying, there can be little doubt that it is a contributing factor when we consider that bullying is one of the main contributing or substantive factors in the suicide of children and young adults.

On July 30, 2010, Kevin Morrissey, managing editor at the University of Virginia literacy magazine Virginia Quarterly Review, shot himself. Warnings and red flags to university officials by coworkers and Morrissey's sister went unheeded.

It was reported that Morrissey placed at least eighteen calls to university officials in the final two weeks of his life.

In France there is an ongoing criminal investigation into allegations that management practices at France Telecom now Orange France led several employees to commit suicide in recent years. The suicide rate at the telecommunications giant exceeds the national average. The probe is looking into a single case and will determine whether France Telecom and one of its managers could be brought to trial for involuntary homicide. This case has brought forward the probable connection between workplace bullying and suicide. In July of 2012, authorities placed the former head of France Telecom, Didier Lombard, under formal investigation. Lombard has resigned because of this.

In March of 2014 Orange initiated another investigation on the suicides of ten employees since the beginning of the year. Most of the reasons were "explicitly related to their jobs.

In July of 2014 Michael Talbot and Avery Hains of Toronto's CTV broadcast of a three part investigation that reported the suicides of two Toronto Police officers who suffered from Post Traumatic Stress Disorder. According to former Staff Sargent Simon Fraser more officers will die because of being bullied into keeping their PTSD hidden.

Not Just Another Statistic

A new study by Joel Goh, a Harvard Associate Professor, finds that more than 120,000 deaths may be attributable to workplace stress. This was nowhere more overt than on January 26th 2015, when Phillip Perea, a former Fox News promotions producer in Austin, Texas fatally shot himself in front of the building in New York which houses the Fox headquarters.

Just before he committed suicide, Perea posted his final grievances against Fox News which linked one of his over 30 YouTube videos over the last few months airing his complaints against Fox. AOL News reported that the videos in 'The American Workplace Bully: How Fox News Ended My Career', paint the picture of a "disgruntled" employee who he believes was outed as part of a master plot against him.

Based on the absence of coverage this story has received, it is apparent that the media, including Fox, accepts the assessment that Perea was "disgruntled" and became unhinged. Because of the lack of analysis and coverage, he becomes just another statistic!

This silence by the media is troublesome and unfortunate as much can be learned from this.

After reading the various reports of the suicide and listening to the many hours of postings Perea made over the last few months, I am convinced that his tragic end could have been avoided.

One in four adults have a mental health condition. Most, with proper diagnosis and treatment can lead healthy, active, productive and satisfying lives. All too many, however, do not recognize what is happening to them and many of those who do, do not seek the help they need. Coping with workplace stress is particularly difficult for people who have an untreated mental health condition. Most organizations are not properly equipped to deal with those who have trouble coping. Also in many instances workplace cultures trigger an existing mental health condition or create one. Most who are bullied at work, suffer from Post Traumatic Stress Disorder (PTSD). Unfortunately the organizational response is to "get rid of the problem".

In Perea's extensive chronicles, he comes across as a troubled, difficult, frustrated and spiteful employee who uses bullying tactics to make his case that he is a victim. What is difficult to determine is what gave rise to the problems he faced at work. In my view, when people try to deal with bullying situations alone they usually fall into a trap, going from a solid employee to a poor performer with a bad attitude, becoming the villain. Perea may have fallen into the trap.

Fox News reported that Perea was with the organization for 10 months suggesting that he may have been a poor hire. No mention is made of the fact that prior to joining the Austin affiliate he worked at their Seattle affiliate, and during his time there he was nominated for several regional Emmy awards. It is very possible that Perea's problems existed before he transferred to Austin.

Based on the secret tapes made by Perea of disciplinary meetings, it appears that local management tried to help him. One of the critical issues raised (without specifics) was a concern by management, that Perea made other workers uncomfortable and fearful. At this point local management should have elevated the situation to corporate headquarters and sought professional help. Perea did indicate an Attention Deficit Disorder (ADD), however, it is now apparent that he suffered from something far more serious and required more help than what local management could provide.

Perea is not just a statistic. He committed suicide, perhaps because, as he claims, he was bullied. If that is the case, a crime has been committed and the organization and or the bullies need to be held accountable. Local management may have been the bullies, if not, they need to be exonerated from the charges leveled against them by Perea. But what were the indicators that Perea was a danger to himself and others?

This sad story needs to be told. Fox News would be well advised to commission an independent investigation in the matter to answer some of the questions raised. By doing so, what is learned here can avoid catastrophic outcomes there and elsewhere and help organizations properly deal with similar situations.

Workplace Bullying and Post Traumatic Stress Disorder (PTSD)

The German Psychotherapist Dr. Heinz Leymann found that people who had been relentlessly bullied at work suffered more intense and persistent Post Traumatic Stress Disorder (PTSD) than train conductors who witnessed suicides by people throwing themselves in front of the train. He discovered that PTSD is probably the correct psychiatric and psychological diagnosis for an astounding 95 percent of the targets of bullying. In an article in the European Journal of Work and Organizational Psychology, Dr. Leymann and Annelie Gustafsson found the train operators' symptoms to be "very much milder" than all of the targets in their workplace bullying study. Also, the proportion of these train drivers who suffer PTSD and share the severe diagnosis was much smaller. In fact, the authors found that the reactions of targets of bullying compare more closely with a Norwegian study concerning raped women.

The core elements of PTSD include captivity or entrapment, psychological fragmentation, the loss of a sense of safety, trust, and self worth, as well as the tendency to be re-victimized. It is not difficult to see how these elements are at play in the workplace. There is certainly a sense of captivity or entrapment because people are usually dependent on their employment for their livelihood. Many adults spend more time at work than they do with their families, or sleeping, so it is understandable that the psychological impact of being bullied includes the loss of a sense of safety, trust and self worth. Usually workplace bullying is repeated and ongoing, which stands to reason that the target goes through the sense of re-victimization, because they are being re-targeted. And if the organization handles the situation poorly, they will once again be re-targeted.

Leymann points out that the train drivers did not experience a series of ongoing further traumatizing rights violations or identity insults from different societal sources such as the raped women and bullied employees. "Mobbing [bullying] and expulsion from the labor market are in themselves a series of victimizations of traumatic strength…torn out of their social network, a life of early retirement with permanent psychological damage threatens the great majority of mobbing victims."

They found that many of the targets of bullying experienced mental effects fully comparable with PTSD from war or prison camp experiences.

A number of serious health conditions, both psychological and physical, can accompany PTSD:

- "depression
- obsession
- agitation
- blockage of the memory of the events
- a resigned attitude
- moderate cognitive disturbances
- automatically recurring thoughts
- irritability
- inner unrest
- panic/anxiety attacks
- hyposomnia
- addiction

- suicidal ideation, thoughts, plans, and attempts
- gastro-intestinal disturbances
- muscular disorders
- chronic muscle hypertension"

Given these symptoms, it is no small wonder that the performance of people who are targeted deteriorates and they are viewed as having a poor attitude and insubordinate. They suffer the symptoms of PTSD, giving the bully the ammunition for continued bullying.

While there are presently no quantitative studies measuring the relationship between divorce and PTSD as a result of bullying, from the abundant anecdotal data available it is clear that marital breakdown is often one of the casualties of being bullied. Thus the target is even more alone with even less of a support structure, and more of the guilt and hurt.

Case Study—A Father's Confession— Tim's Story

In 2010 Tim's Dad, Fred, called him to come to his place as soon as possible. "I don't have much time left and I have a confession to make before I go," was his sombre plea.

At twenty-five Tim was the eldest of Fred's three children. Fred left his wife Mary eight years before and lived with his elderly mother, who was the only person who would have him. Fred was an unemployed alcoholic and he had very little contact with his family in the eight years since he left. Tim recalls Fred's drinking problem started around ten years ago when Tim was fifteen and suspected that it was related to Fred being fired from his position as CFO of a Canadian retailer in 1998. In the few years before he left Fred was verbally and physically abusive to everyone in the family.

While Tim was civil whenever he had contact with Fred, he resented him for leaving and he considered Fred a loser. Andrea and Jim, Tim's brother and sister, were more charitable in their feelings towards Fred, as was Mary. She regularly sent Fred's mother a check to help her out with the expenses as she knew Fred had no income and her mother in-law was not in a financial position to support him.

Fred was in a lot of pain; Tim could tell when they met. Fred told Tim the whole story, and by the time he was finished Tim felt both outrage and regret. Outrage for what happened to his dad and regret on how he treated and misjudged him.

Fred joined the company in 1987 as a comptroller and was promoted to CFO in 1996, reporting to Janice the CEO. Janice was a very demanding boss, but because of his performance and capabilities, Fred did not suffer the abuse Janice doled out on a regular basis to others in the organization.

In August of 1997 Fred was offered a CFO position with a larger retailer. When he advised Janice he was leaving, she begged him to reconsider, giving him a huge raise, a staying bonus and a promise that he would be considered for her replacement in a few years' time. Fred reconsidered and decided to stay.

A month after he decided to stay, Janice started to ride Fred, criticising almost everything that he did. The emails from Janice were endless, every day, at all hours, weekends and holidays. Everything was ASAP and Janice expected immediate responses, and if he did not respond immediately, she would send another. Janice started excluding Fred from critical meetings, did not communicate decisions she had made and started dealing directly with one of Fred's subordinates without involving him.

All of this started to erode Fred's confidence and as a result his performance. He did not know how to handle the situation. This is when he started to drink heavily, which led to the downward spiral. As a result of the stress and the drinking, Fred gained weight and started having heart problems.

The harassment and abuse lasted eleven months. In August of 1999, exactly a year after Fred told Janice he was leaving, Janice fired Fred "for cause," citing his poor performance over the last year. Her parting comment was, "Nobody quits on me!"

Fred sought legal advice and the lawyer indicated to him that Janice had built up a very good case for terminating him and advised him to accept the three months severance that Janice had offered. Feeling he had no choice Fred accepted the offer.

Totally broken, unfit, and an alcoholic, Fred was not able to find new employment. Janice blacklisted Fred by discrediting him in the industry. Having told the story to Tim, Fred felt a great relief.

It was the first time he had confided to anyone about what he had gone through, because he was ashamed. His health had deteriorated to the point that he had only weeks to live and he wanted to make things right and confess and apologize to his family, and he chose Tim as the conduit.

Author's note

Fred passed away five weeks later. Believing he was at fault rather than the victim was the major reason for his downfall, which happens with all too many targets. There is no question that Fred suffered from PTSD, and if he had not dealt with what he went through alone, or those who were close to him recognized the symptoms and intervened, Fred would be alive today.

I can clearly relate to what Fred went through as I was bullied and retaliated against because I blew the whistle and exposed a corrupt executive. While I am unable to relate my story—in my case I am bound by a nondisclosure agreement—I am able to tell the stories of others like Fred who had been negatively impacted because of bullying in the work place.

For me the experience was physically and emotionally debilitating. Also, for too long I was made to believe that I was the culprit; my self-confidence was destroyed and my relationship with family, friends, and associates was severely tested. I fell into what I call the *"The Bully's Trap,"* which, I have discovered, is all too common with people who are targeted.

Part Three

Effectively Dealing
With The Issue

"Knowing what's right doesn't mean
much unless you do what's right"

—Theodore Roosevelt

The Barriers

Bullying cannot be stopped by the ineffective techniques commonly used by human resource people. Sensitivity and diversity training, conflict resolution techniques and sending the bully to charm school do not work.

Bullying is a systemic problem. In most cases, the focus is either on the bully or the target rather than on the culture and where there is an intervention. It should also include an intervention in the culture of the organization.

There are five main obstacles to stopping this bullying:

1. Fear—Bullying is rarely reported by either the bullied or the bystander.

   • Those who do report are usually labelled "disgruntled employees" or "trouble makers," and are discredited and retaliated against.

   • Those who leave the organization because of bullying and/or whistle blowing often find they are blacklisted and have difficulty finding alternate employment.

2. Awareness and Concern

   • Awareness: as with targets, bystanders may be unaware that what they are observing is bullying. Even if they can identify the actions and behaviors as bullying they may not be aware of what they can do to help the target.

- Concern: lack of concern on the part of bystanders is a more difficult problem. This lack of concern may be because of their own insensitivity or callousness, or it could be because they have sided with the bully and/ or feel it in their best interest to care more about their wellbeing than the person being targeted. If the target goes down, they may benefit from this.

3. The Attitudes and Behaviors of Leaders

- CEO is also the CBO (Chief Bullying Officer)— Bosses are the bullies in over 70 percent of the reported incidents.

- Leaders who do not view verbal or psychological abuse as violence or do not make the connection that these

- types of predatory aggressions can give rise to the physical aggression.

- Leaders who like bullies because they believe bullies get things done and are high performers. In many situations the CEO is also the CBO (Chief Bullying Officer).

- Leaders who think employees will abuse workplace violence—harassment legislation, policies and procedures. They fear that any intervention to correct deficiencies will be considered harassment. In 2010 Michael Bloomberg, the former Mayor of New York City, warned that if the State of New York passed proposed legislation, many companies will move their work to New Jersey. He as much said: "If we don't allow companies to abuse employees, they will be uncompetitive!"

4. Organizational Response

- Ignoring the problem or retaliating against the target. In the majority of cases where abuse was reported to the employer, the employer ignored the problem or made the problem worse by retaliating against the target.
- Labeling a bullying situation as a personality clash, or an aggressive management style.
- Applying conflict resolution techniques, which makes the situation worse for the target.

5. Governance

- Boards of Directors that do not monitor or audit cultural factors of an organization or have appropriate checks and balances in place to predict and identify bullying.

Many jurisdictions have workplace violence and/or harassment legislation. Where there is legislation it is estimated that there is a 30 percent compliance rate. Some organizations that put policies, procedures and programs in place do so to be legally compliant, not necessarily to stop the bullying. Workplace bullying and serious organizational problems go hand in hand.

In my experience, where bullying occurs, the following dynamics are usually at play:

- Leaders score very low on the respectability scale.
- Fear is used as a substitute for motivation and positive leadership.
- There is a disproportionate focus on the short term, at the expense of sustainable long-term performance.

- Leaders do not appreciate the risks to brand and reputational value when bullying is exposed.

- Leaders condone lax ethical standards.

- People are considered expendable.

- There is subjectivity and ambiguity in performance management and advancement.

- Individual performance is rewarded over team performance.

- There are few checks and balances.

- Contrary viewpoints or opinions are not welcome.

- There is negligence at the governance level.

As I have asserted in Part One, workplace bullying is part of a larger systemic issue that requires a systemic change. For bullying to stop, it requires a cultural change that is culturally and organizationally centered.

Bullying and the Attraction and Retention of Talent

A ttraction and retention of talent will become the biggest catalyst for organizations to ensure that their workplaces are safe and free from bullying.

I have worked with a number of companies in a variety of sectors across North America on cultural transformation. For many, what triggered the initiative was the ability to attract and retain talent. Many wanted to build on cultures to establish themselves as the organization of choice, for both customers and employees. One bank I worked with has as their number one initiative establishing the firm as the firm of choice for women with wealth and women in wealth.

Within five years, the attraction and retention of talent will emerge as the biggest challenge for employers. This is already the case in some sectors, health care and technology, as examples.

Notwithstanding the current levels of unemployment, demographics dictate that the participation rate will decrease at a greater rate than the demand for employees in most sectors and categories of employees.

In addition to the lower participation rate, research is showing that the defection rate will dramatically rise. A 2010 survey of British workers indicates that an astounding 50 percent want to leave their current organization when the economy turns around—the main reason, conflict with their boss or coworker (read: bullying). Realistically not all of the 50 percent are going to defect, but the extent of the discontent is disturbing.

One organization I worked with had great difficulty convincing search firms to recruit for them because the organization had a terrible reputation, where bullying was not only condoned, it was encouraged.

As part of the cultural transformation process, I encourage organizations to develop a Value Exchange Model (based on the Ethic of Reciprocity) with the various employee categories. In retail the Value Exchange Model with customers is widely used by the tier one retailers. This model is understanding and delivering on the expectations that each have of each other.

Factoring Bullying into the Being Hired / Hiring Equation

Given that there will be more choices for people when they decide to change employment, the cultures of prospective employers will become a major factor.

In making a decision whether to change employers, I encourage people to conduct a thorough due diligence and avoid going from a known situation to one that is an unknown and potentially toxic. In "Pam's Story—Onto Pleasure Island" I relay what happened to Pam when she left a positive situation after nine successful years and found herself in a totally toxic one. Had Pam done better due diligence she could have avoided what became a living nightmare that continues to haunt her.

When considering a change I recommend the following:

1. *Understand what you are leaving.*

   For over 70 percent of those who are bullied, the only way to stop the bullying is to quit. You do not have to quit to have the bullying stop, and if this is the main or only reason, you should consider your options.

2. *Have the search firm/recruiter consider you an equal client.*

The search firm/recruiter has the inside knowledge of the organization and should be able to answer questions regarding the culture and history of the organization and its people.

While the organization is the paying client, potential and successful candidates must be considered equal as clients. Part of what the search firm must do is properly and honestly make people aware of what they are getting into, and be held accountable if they misrepresent the situation and, as in Pam's case, if it does not work out, providing the ability to seek legal recourse.

3. *Find out as much as you can about the organization.*

Talk to people you know in the organization. If you don't know anyone, as part of the recruitment process ask to have access to two or three people who will give candid input. Being able to speak to the person you are replacing will provide valuable insight. If you know former employees of the organization, they will likely be more comfortable being candid.

Check the Internet for any media reports related to bullying/violence, sexual harassment, human rights claims, class action lawsuits, reported or alleged wrongdoings, and union certification drives.

Talk to people external to the organization. Vendors and clients you may know will have insights and viewpoints that can help you assess.

4. *Questions you should be asking.*

- What are the values and operating principles, and how are they applied?

- What are the characteristics of the culture in the organization? (See section "What's Culture Got To Do With It.")

- Who am I replacing? And if that person left, how long was she with the organization and in the position and why did she leave?

- What is the turnover rate in the organization and the department?

- Are exit interviews conducted? What are the reasons people cited for leaving?

- Why is this an external hire?

- As part of the hiring and advancement to management processes, are psychological assessments conducted? (If the answer to this one is no—beware!)

- What is the investment in management and leadership training?

- Do regions and/or departments operate on an integrated basis or as silos?

- Describe the performance management system. What gets measured? What's the balance between individual and team? To what extent are performance reviews two-way discussions?

- Do terms of engagement exist for resolving differences and disputes?

- Are there policies, procedures and practices in place relating to code of conduct and conflict of interest?

- What are the highlights of the latest employee attitude / engagement survey? What was the participation rate in the latest survey?

- Is employee absenteeism a problem?

- What did the organization do to minimize the negative impact on people during the economic downturn?

- Are contrarian viewpoints welcome?

- In terms of organizational priorities, where does talent rank? In the annual plan what are the specific initiatives in place that focus on talent as a priority?

5. *Find out as much as you can about the person you will be reporting to.*

  - Tenure with the organization and in the position
  - Style
  - Personality
  - Any history of harassment or bullying
  - Relationship with people in the department
  - Relationship with the person you are replacing

  In assessing the organization's culture, try to connect all of the information and look for any inconsistencies. If there are inconsistencies, seek clarification.

6. *Be honest about why you are making the change.*
  You will be asked why you are making a change. If the reason you are leaving your current employer is to stop the bullying, you don't have to get into the gory details. You can simply state that your values do not align with those of the organization.

Attraction and retention of talent should be one of the top priorities in every organization. The culture of the organization, or put another way, what the organization stands for and how it operates is the biggest factor in why people decide to join and stay.

In the event you run into resistance, receive vague responses, or there are inconsistencies in the responses, consider these to be indicators of the culture that exists. The recruiter in enticing you to join will try to sell, and understandably accentuate the positive. If you are informed, you will be able to determine if what is portrayed is either real or not.

I also advise you to take notes of all of the conversations you have during the hiring process. This record will help you seek recourse if there has been a misrepresentation and the move ends badly.

Is There a Psychopath in the House?

As with most issues there is rarely a magic bullet to resolve the problem. Bullying in the workplace is no exception. As I have previously stated to stop bullying from occurring it takes a comprehensive, integrated approach. There is one thing, however, that comes close to being a magic bullet, which is for organizations to make mandatory a psychological test for anyone who is being hired or promoted to a management or supervisory position.

A highly regarded psychologist, Robert Hare, developed a checklist of twenty telltale signs that help detect whether someone is a psychopath—being a predator who uses charm, manipulation, intimidation, sex and violence to control others and to satisfy their own selfish needs. This description matches many of the bullies that I have profiled. Hare is convinced many important CEOs and politicians fall into this category.

Dean Haycock, PhD summarized the twenty telltale signs developed by Hare as follows:

- "glib and superficial charm
- grandiose (exaggeratedly high) estimation of self
- need for stimulation
- pathological lying
- cunning and manipulative
- lack of remorse or guilt
- shallow affect (superficial emotional responsiveness)

- callousness and lack of empathy
- parasitic lifestyle
- poor behavioral controls
- sexual promiscuity
- early behavioral problems
- lack of realistic long term goals
- impulsivity
- failure to accept responsibility for own actions
- many short-term marital relationships
- juvenile delinquency
- revocation of conditional release
- criminal versatility"

Organizations should rely on professionals like industrial psychologists to make the assessments.

Case Study—I Flunked The Test And They Still Hired Me!—Andrew's Story

One company, a conglomerate of a number of related business units I worked with, has had a psychological assessment as part of its hiring and advancement protocol for over two decades. This company had the characteristics of a Stable culture. The CEO decided to retire after a very successful twelve-year run as CEO. The selection committee of the board established the criteria for the new CEO and they placed a heavy emphasis on bringing in a change agent, someone who had the experience and background to reinvent the company. While the company was very successful in the past, market conditions and new competition threatened the sustainability of revenue and earnings growth.

After an extensive and long international search process, the search committee identified an individual who looked like a perfect match to the profile established. On paper Andrew was by far the most qualified of any of the other candidates. He interviewed well and he was a recognized change agent having turned around three major organizations in the last fifteen years. As is the case when attracting someone away from other organization, it was difficult to obtain direct references. Those that the executive recruiter was able to get were positive, particularly regarding Andrew's background and experience. One common theme, however, was that Andrew was very demanding and "does not suffer fools lightly."

When Andrew was told that he had to go through a psychological assessment before an offer was made, he reacted by indicating that he viewed this as insulting and threatened to withdraw from the running. The executive recruiter, after much persuasion, convinced Andrew to have the assessment done, indicating to him that this was a long-standing protocol, and there were no exemptions. Andrew was also told not to worry about it, it was just a process that the head of human resources insisted on, and the selection committee had already made up their mind, regardless of the results of the assessment.

John, an industrial psychologist, has been doing the testing and interviews with candidates for management positions with the company for the last seven years, with an incredible track record. The company only hired or promoted people who John felt would be successful in the culture. The management team were considered to be the best and the brightest in the industry. Turnover of staff was very low. On the annual engagement surveys, the scores for leadership, communication and being treated with respect were always higher than the benchmark of other companies. The performance and productivity metrics over the last ten years exceeded those of benchmark companies in the industry, worldwide.

When John administered the test and interviewed Andrew he knew almost from the outset that Andrew would not be a good fit. While Andrew was obviously on his best behavior during the interviews, with John he was defensive, mocked the process and declared, "When I become the CEO, you won't be doing much work with us." The assessment concluded that Andrew was close to being a psychopath.

John presented his findings to the head of human resources, the chair of the selection committee and the executive recruiter. Both the executive recruiter and the head of the selection committee rejected John's assessment. The executive recruiter discredited John by indicating he had a reputation in the industry for not being objective and did not like people who were demanding and tough. The head of human resources argued that John's track record was solid. The chair of the selection committee argued that the criteria they had established called for a change agent and "to make the changes that need to be done, we need one tough bastard." At the insistence of the head of human resources John's report was submitted to the selection committee and then to the full board.

The board was clearly divided. Most felt uncomfortable in making an offer given the report. However, the head of the selection committee made a strong argument citing the need for "one tough bastard," and he also reminded them that there was no strong alternative and that the board was under tremendous pressure from shareholders to name a CEO. After much debate a decision was make to make an offer to Andrew, which he accepted. No reference to the assessment was made.

What John outlined in his report proved to be accurate. According to the head of human resources, Andrew's behavior was far worse than what he anticipated knowing what was in the report. Within one year from Andrew's date of hire the culture went from Stable to Dictatorial. Eight of the twelve members of the senior management team resigned, including the head of human resources. Andrew brought in people (all male) that worked for him at his previous companies to replace those who left. They became Andrew's henchmen. Relationships with employees and vendors deteriorated. Fault lines were starting to show, all of the performance metrics were on a downward trend. Andrew tried to force the CFO to report inflated revenue and profit numbers. The CFO refused and Andrew fired her for insubordination. She was given a huge severance, with the understanding that she would not reveal to anyone the events surrounding her termination. The board was clueless as to what was going on. Two years into his tenure, Andrew knew that he could only hide the inevitable for so long, so he decided that rather than reinvent the company and grow it, the better option was to divest any part that was not core. The board bought into this strategy and 80 percent of the business was sold for what most, who knew what the potential was, too low a multiple. The board considered Andrew a hero for avoiding what they thought was a potential long-term disaster, and gave him a multi-million dollar incentive for successfully dismantling the company. Andrew also triggered the change of control provision in his agreement (which stipulated that if over 50 percent of the company were sold, a multi- million dollar severance would be paid).

All of the businesses that were sold turned into great acquisitions and solid performers, validating what those in the know were representing—that they were sold at too low a multiple.

Author's Note

Andrew went on to become CEO of another major organization whose performance started to significantly deteriorate a year and a half after Andrew became its "leader."

The decline and fall of this company could have been avoided had the board taken the psychological assessment seriously.

Again, over 70 percent of bullying is boss to subordinate. Not hiring or promoting a bully to a position of power reduces the risk of bullying. Having a scientifically proven method to identify bullies is close to a magic bullet to stop bullying from occurring, and I highly recommend that all organizations make a psychological assessment part of their hiring for and promotion to management protocol.

Part Four

Guidance and Advice

"Never give in, never give in, never, never, never, never—
in nothing, great or small in except to conviction of
honour and good sense never yield to force: never yield
to the apparently overwhelming might of the enemy."

—Winston Churchill

Overcoming It—
Advice to The Bullied

"Although the world is full of suffering,
it is full also of the overcoming of it."

—Helen Keller

In most cases of bullying in the workplace, people allow it to happen, do not report it and try to deal with it on their own. Research shows that for over 70 percent the only way for the bullying to stop is to quit. When this happens the bully has clearly won and will very likely find a new target.

People react to bullying in different ways. Some just let it happen, others get angry and retaliate, some become bullies and take out their anger on others (often their families), and others revert to extreme measures such as seriously injuring or killing the people that they feel are responsible for their being bullied and for others, the only way out for them is to commit (or attempt) suicide.

It is my belief that people who are being bullied can do something about it in a positive and safe way, which for them will have a positive outcome.

There is no set formula or step-by-step process. What I offer is a number of points which should be used as a guide. Also, the approach taken should vary based on the organizational culture, e.g., in a "Stable" culture, I encourage people to follow the process prescribed by the organization, because there the officials, usually Human Resources, can be trusted to act in the best interest of the person being bullied. Conversely, in a "Dictatorial" culture, I recommend that people deal with their situation outside the process prescribed by the organization, because there the officials, again usually Human Resources, should be viewed with scepticism, as they either have zero influence to stop the bullying, or they are part of the problem. In what I describe as a "Disjointed" culture, I advise caution on whether to follow the process prescribed by the organization, and suggest only going to an internal official that they have absolute trust in.

Much can be learned from the experiences of others. Bullying is not a one-off situation. Bullying in an organization or by an individual usually follows a pattern. People in an organization are usually aware of others who have been bullied in the past. Reaching out to these people and having them relate their experiences will provide valuable insight on what to do, and what to avoid, and who to trust.

If you are being bullied, I offer the following on what to do (and not do.)

1. *Don't deal with it alone*

> "Trouble is part of your life, and if you don't share it, you don't give the person who loves you a chance to love you enough."
>
> —Dinah Shore

Talk to someone who is close to you about it. This is not something you should be ashamed of. You are not the first and only person dealing with this. It is not your fault. People you are close to want to help you and can help you through this. You need someone to help you think through the steps we offer, challenge you and help you develop a strategy.

Don't hide the situation from your family; they need to know, as they can also indirectly be victims. Also, they will know something is wrong and will observe things about you that you may not be aware of- mood swings, disengagement, irritability etc. If they are aware of what you are going through they can not only help you through it, they can help you build your sense of self, which I believe is a prerequisite for taking an assertive position.

2. *Build your "Sense of Self"*

"No one can make you feel inferior without your consent."

—Eleanor Roosevelt

Accept the fact that the bully wants to break you. Don't succumb to it! If you are being bullied at work it takes over your life, it becomes your life, and it will lower your sense of self.

Understand who you are and what you offer- at home, in your community and at work. Many people withdraw from whom they are when they are bullied. Do the opposite- become a better spouse, parent, son, daughter, friend, coach, mentor, volunteer, expert and producer. Feeling good about who you are, what you do and what you offer will help you avoid the bullying from taking over your life. Exercise and the right diet are helpful in building on your sense of self when you go through this trauma.

Having this strong sense of self will also put you in a better frame of mind to deal with the bullying.

3. *Don't become a bully who is targeted by another bully*

A bully who is targeted by another bully is both a target and a bully. In what I call a Dictatorial culture the CEO is usually a CBO who bullies his direct reports, who in turn bully the front line managers, who in turn bully the front line employees.

Dictatorial and Disjointed cultures are usually full of bullies who are targeted by other bullies. Often in these cultures people feel it is the only way to survive. They feel forced to behave in a manner that is inconsistent with their values and beliefs. Regardless of the culture in your organization, you can not only survive, you can excel by staying true to your values and beliefs and treating people with respect and dignity. By doing this you will garner the respect, loyalty and support of your peers and subordinates. Also, by doing this you will be a role model for others who are being bullied. From my perspective, there is no better way to build on your sense of self than to be above it all and not allow yourself to act and behave inconsistently with your value system.

Reacting this way to being bullied is the most respectful form of revolt, and one that even the most powerful of bullies will have difficulty discrediting. As Mark Twain wrote, "Fewer things are harder to put up with than the annoyance of a good example."

4. *Validate the bullying*

> "The man who is swimming against the stream knows the strength of it."
>
> —Woodrow Wilson

Organizations have the right to discipline, demote and fire. As outlined earlier there are many ways and means of bullying. You may be discriminated against, but that does not necessarily constitute bullying. You may be teased, but that does not necessarily mean you are being bullied. You may be confronted, someone may flirt with you, you may be subject to an incident of impulsive aggression, but again these acts do not necessarily constitute bullying. Understanding what bullying is and what it is not and making distinctions (see "Making Distinctions") will help validate whether or not bullying is occurring.

Validating in your own mind that bullying is occurring will put you on the offense rather than the defense when you decide to confront the situation. Bullies when confronted usually will say things like: "You are taking it the wrong way," "I don't mean to harm," "I'm passionate about the company and sometimes get carried away because of my passion," and "That's my style and I am only doing what is expected of me to improve performance."

You must be ready for these pat answers by saying things like, "I understand, but these actions and behaviors constitute bullying."

Bullying is usually not one act. Bullies can be very subtle and manipulative and utilize a combination of a number of forms and ways of bullying. It is therefore important to tie seemingly unrelated comments, events and situations together to fully outline and put into context what is happening to you.

5. *Understand what is motivating the bullying*

As indicated earlier the primary reasons employees are targeted, are;

- Retaliation
- Bigotry
- Exploitation
- Abuse of power
- Eliminating a threat

Knowing why you are being targeted will help you challenge the situation. Again, being able to assert or indicate that you strongly believe that you are being targeted will put you on the offense rather than on the defense. You are not likely the first or only target, and as such whoever is dealing with the situation will not be able to ignore your assertion or belief. This combined with the actions and behaviors of the bully gives you credibility, particularly if the person dealing with it relates it to other like situations he or she is aware of.

6. *Keep a detailed diary of what you are going through*

By documenting every comment, situation and event you will be better able to not only fully analyze what you are going through, you will be better able to state your position. Bullies discredit their targets. By having the facts, properly framed and marshalled, you will be able to turn the situation around by discrediting the bully. For obvious reasons bullies do not keep a running record of their actions and behaviors.

Bullies need to know that they will be held accountable for "creating unfavorable impressions," that are not true.

Record conversations you have with the bully. Small recorders that look like a pen are available at most electronic stores (some with video cameras are also available). Proof of these conversations proving abusive or threatening language will add credibility to your position. The bully may claim that recording the conversation is illegal; you counter that the bully's behavior is the illegal action here. It is not illegal to tape record a conversation as long as one of the parties are aware. You are one of the parties.

7. *Don't fall into The Bully's Trap*

"I learned long ago never to wrestle with a pig. You get dirty, and besides the pig likes it."

—Cyrus Ching

As I indicated earlier, bullies try to discredit their targets. The usual criticisms they lodge include deteriorating performance, poor attitude, insubordination and ironically enough poor people skills. While bullies don't document their actions and behaviors, rest assured that they will be documenting yours to build up a case against you. The advice is; don't fall into this trap.

I know it will not be easy, but, rather than allow being bullied to affect your performance or attitude, focus on excelling, keep your anger in check, and don't get sucked into a confrontation with the bully.

8. *Don't get set-up*

There are different ways and means of bullying. Bullies use tactics such as excluding you from essential meetings, giving you the wrong time for meetings to start, having you prepare for a topic different than what will be addressed, setting unreasonable expectations and measuring your performance based on subjectivity and ambiguity. Having clarity around meetings, timing of meetings, agendas, expectations, and what you are measured on will help you avoid getting set up.

Be assertive, get written confirmation on anything that the bully could set you up on. If you are not invited to a meeting that you should be at, go to the meeting anyway. If you are not receiving correspondence or reports that you should be getting, figure out a way to get them. The message here is to be sensitive to everything that is going on and be one or two steps ahead of the bully.

9. *Call the Bully on it*

Timing is key here. At the earliest opportunity you should make this request. Ideally the first step is to simply indicate to the bully that you do not appreciate being bullied and ask that it be stopped. Do it in a respectful manner. Don't get into a debate. Just indicate that you know that you are being bullied and want it to stop. Bullies are not used to being called on their actions and behaviors. This direct request could possibly disarm him and have the bullying stop.

If the bully wants to debate the issue, indicate that you are happy to do so, but you want a witness present. The witness should either be the bully's immediate superior or a human resource representative. Having a detailed diary of the comments, events and situations helps you control the situation.

At this session, do not accept rationalizations like this is a style issue or a personality clash. Also, don't accept a conflict resolution approach, because this suggests that you are in a fight with the bully. Bullying is not a fight; it takes two or more to fight. Bullying is one sided and you are on the receiving end. The purpose of the session is to register your expectation that the bullying stop. You should also put them on notice that if the bullying does not stop and / or you are retaliated against because you made this request you will take further steps.

If the bullying persists and/or you are being retaliated against, register your complaint with someone in the organization you have absolute trust in. In a Stable culture it should be the head of human resources, in a Dictatorial or Disjointed culture it could be the person in charge of legal or internal audit.

"A fox should not be the jury at a goose's trial."

—Thomas Fuller

If the organization initiates an investigation, make sure you sign off on how the investigation will be conducted and who will be interviewed. You should be assured that the investigation will not become a "kangaroo court," where a disproportionate focus of the investigation is on you. In the section "Human Resources part of the problem or part of the solution" I provide advice to human resource people on conducting investigations involving bullying.

10. *Get professional help*

If you believe that you are being set up to be fired or you have lost control of the situation, seek advice from an employment lawyer, or if you are represented by a union, your union representative. Armed with your detailed diary you will get professional advice on what your legal options are. Courts are becoming less tolerant of employers who condone and/or encourage bullying. Remember, if you have your facts properly framed and marshalled, you are in a better position to take control, or regain control of the situation, this time by involving external help and potentially seeking legal recourse.

Research shows that most of the people who are bullied suffer from "Post Traumatic Stress Disorder." The stress of being bullied can and does affect your physical and mental health. In some cases it can lead people to take drastic action, the most extreme being murder and suicide. Like my first point, "Don't deal with it alone," if you are having symptoms don't deal with it alone, seek psychological help. Remember, there should be no shame in what you are going through, and it is not your fault. If you don't properly deal with the symptoms, you will allow the situation to control you and it could lead to an extremely bad outcome.

11. *Help start the revolution for change*

"A good indignation brings out all one's powers."

—Ralph Waldo Emerson

You as a bullied employee are also very likely a bystander, particularly if you work in a Dictatorial or Disjointed culture. Having been bullied and being in control of the situation and stopping it, you are in a powerful position to change it. While I have cautioned against anger, I encourage indignation, and this indignation against what you went through should also carry forward to what others in the organization are going through.

"Let us not look back in anger or forward in fear, but around in awareness."

—James Thurber

Defining the Unjust—
Advice to the Bystander

First they came for the communists, and I didn't speak
out because I wasn't a communist. Then they came
for the trade unionists, and I didn't speak out because
I wasn't a trade unionist. Then they came for the Jews,
and I didn't speak out because I wasn't a Jew. Then they
came for me and there was no one left to speak for me.

—Marten Niemollers

I n the course of your working career, you will be exposed to
bullying and be a bystander. When this happens, you have
to make choices—do nothing, actively or passively support the
bully, or become a witness and/or defender and or a resistor.

Choosing to be a witness, a defender or a resistor is not free of
risk; this requires courage. Choosing not to be a witness, defender,
or resistor is also not free of risk when you consider:

- Could I have helped avoid a physical or mental breakdown?
- Could I have helped avoid ruining a career?
- Could I have helped avoid a family breakdown?
- Could I have helped avoid the organization's downfall?
- Could I have helped avoid a suicide (or attempted suicide)?
- Could I have helped avoid a murder?

All of these are real risks that I believe outweigh the risk of being a witness, defender and resistor.

In making this choice, knowing there is risk, the way you handle it will help minimize the risk to you and the target. Do not be impulsive or reckless. What you do must be fact based. Handle the situation with great sensitivity, tact and respect.

I offer the following advice on how you can help or try to help the target:

1. *Become a witness*

   When you either observe bullying or suspect that someone is being bullied, start taking notes of what you hear and see.

   Even though the bullying may be subtle, there are lots of indicators. The main indicators are how the target reacts to the bullying. (Change in personality, withdrawn, disengaged, lashing out, slippage in performance, higher absenteeism, signs of substance abuse, negative comments about the organization and management, and other behaviors or comments that are uncharacteristic.)

   The other indicators include comments made by other bystanders, the water cooler chit chat, gossip, comments made by the bully (remember the bully is intent on discrediting the target), and the target being excluded from situations and correspondence that he / she would normally be part of. As this is likely not the bully's first target, recalling previous situations you are aware of and comparing them to this situation can reveal other indicators.

   As in my advice to the bullied by having facts properly framed and marshalled, if you register that bullying is occurring, your evidence will carry a lot of weight. Remember, bullies are unlikely to keep a running record of their actions and behaviors.

2. *Validate the bullying*

We have outlined what constitutes bullying and what doesn't. Organizations have the right to discipline, demote and fire. You may have a legitimate reason to challenge these decisions, but they do not necessarily constitute bullying. Understanding what bullying is and what it is not and making distinctions like teasing vs. taunting will help validate whether or not bullying is occurring.

Previously I outlined the many forms, ways and means of bullying. Bullies can be very subtle and manipulative and utilize a combination of a number of these forms, ways and means. It is therefore important to tie seemingly unrelated comments, events and situations together to fully outline and put into context what is happening to the target.

3. *Become outraged*

With genocide, the most extreme form of bullying, it went on because too few citizens did not become outraged enough to become witnesses, defenders, resistors or activists. When we become outraged we are more likely to be motivated to correct what we believe is wrong. Had the small percentage of people in Nazi-occupied countries, or in Bosnia, Uganda and other countries been outraged enough with what occurred, the course of history would have been different.

4. *Reach out to the target*

In my advice to the bullied, the first piece of advice I give is, "Don't deal with it alone." The target is in a lonely place and does not believe that there is anyone who can or will help. Go to the target and say, "I think you are being bullied; is there anything I can do to help?" This approach will let the target know they are not alone, and it will also confirm what they suspect. If the target is too ashamed to acknowledge that he is being bullied, relay to him your observations, and if there is a pattern of bullying, indicate that he is not the first target.

5. *Help the target "Build Sense of Self"*
Building a strong sense of self is the prerequisite to be able to control the situation and not be controlled by it.

You are in a unique position to help him do this. Assuming you know the target, you can highlight the positive attributes he has. You can also contrast the positives with what you observe as negative reactions to being bullied and help him make the assessment that his sense of self is being compromised by the bully.

6. *Help the target become assertive*
The first step is point five, helping the target build sense of self. The next steps are helping him to follow points four through nine in "Advice to the Bullied"

• Validate whether you are being bullied.

• Understand what is motivating the bully.

• Keep a detailed diary of what you are going through.

• Don't fall into *The Bully's Trap.*

• Avoid getting set up.

• Make a formal request to have the bullying stop.

All of these are things that usually fall outside of people's comfort zones and as such to help, coach, support and provide constructive criticism is extremely beneficial to the target.

7. *Avoid having the target do harm to himself or others*
If you feel that the target needs professional help, encourage him to seek it. Here you may have to go to the target's family or other friends for a proper intervention.

If you feel that the target has the potential of harming himself or others you must report the situation to someone in authority. In the section "Human Resources—part of the problem or part of the solution," I outline indicators to watch out for. These red flags are always evident, and most extreme examples of violence could have been avoided if there were early intervention. Most leaders do not view verbal or psychological abuse as violence or make the connection that these types of predatory aggression give rise to the physical aggression (by both the bullied and the bully). Fill the void of leadership here and make the connection.

When you report this, you are not being disloyal to the target. You are not a snitch; you are protecting the target and others who potentially could get seriously injured or killed.

8. *Request that the bully stop the bullying*

If the target is not able to handle the situation and you have a solid enough relationship with the bully, indicate that you know what is going on and that it would be in his best interest to stop the bullying. It is advisable to point out that you are on to him through your own observations and that the target did not complain to you.

Alternatively if your relationship with the bully is not solid, but is solid with the bully's immediate superior, make the request that he intervene.

9. *Formally register and report*

If point number eight is not feasible or has backfired on you, you should report the situation to someone in authority that you have absolute trust in. If there is no one you have confidence in to properly intervene and keep it confidential, protecting both you and the target, you should consider two options:

- Submit the report to either the organization's legal counsel or external auditor (with the understanding that you will not be revealed as the source of the report and the target will not be retaliated against)

  or

- Send the report anonymously to the organization's lawyer. If this is the route you take the report should identify the bully and outline as much as you can without identifying you as the source or the target. Also, you should outline your expectation that the matter will be properly investigated and that the bullying stop. If the bullying continues and/or you and the target are subject to retaliation, file a report with the Chair of the board of directors pointing out that the report was sent to the company's lawyer and what happened as a result.

10. *Hold the organization and its leaders accountable*
    When you report you must be very clear on your motivation, which is to have the bullying stop. Without having it sound like blackmail, indicate that if the situation is not properly investigated and the bullying does not stop, or you and the target experience retaliation, that you will take the matter further. (You don't have to say what further is.)

11. *Help start the revolution for change*
    As the bystander you are in a powerful position to change the culture. While I caution against anger, I encourage indignation against what the targets and others in the organization are going through.

12. *Build on your "Sense of Self"*
    Recognize that your choice to become a witness, defender, and activist has significantly strengthened your "Sense of Self"—*Congratulations!*

Redemption— Advice to the Bully

You've got to be brave and you've got to be bold.
Brave enough to take your chance on your own
discrimination—what's right and what's wrong,
what's good and what's bad.

—Robert Frost

My advice to those who bully is simply stop bullying, and change or be changed.

My research shows that the majority of bullies are what I refer to as a bully who is targeted by another bully. These people usually work in cultures that condone, encourage and expect their managers to motivate by fear and intimidation and have CEOs who are also CBOs (Chief Bullying Officers). Many of these people behave outside of their value system, and all too many love to exert their power though bullying. Sadly for many, bullying is the only way they know how to get things done.

Most of the bullies I have dealt with were unhappy people who did not even like themselves and therefore had no problem being mean to others.

One of the purposes of the book is to "help bullies change." In the introduction I outline the eleven things I believe need to happen for bullying to stop.

Regarding the bully, I believe:

- That an employee index be a major component on how managers are measured.

- Bullies need to be held accountable for their behaviors and actions.

- Where workplace bullying is a factor in a suicide, the organization and the bully should face criminal charges.

- Where workplace bullying causes major harm, the organization the bully should face criminal and/or civil charges.

Another purpose of this book is to raise the level of awareness, and by raising the level of awareness, help empower both the target and the bystanders to force the bullying to stop and hold the organization and the bully accountable for their behaviors and actions.

While I raise the level of awareness on the risks and the costs of bullying to the individual, the family unit, the organization, and the community, I found that what really resonates with the bully is the risk they could face.

For me, if the motive for a bully to stop bullying is risk avoidance, that is sufficient, not ideal, but sufficient.

I offer the following advice to the bully:

1. *If you are the CBO (Chief Bullying Officer), really study this book.*

   Unless you change or are changed, your organization will operate in a culture of fear, you will not hear what you need to hear, your organization will not reach its full potential, the best and the brightest will not stay or join and you place your organization at risk. While I believe that bullies in your organization can stop being bullies, if you are a bully it will obviously be difficult for them to do so.

2. *Understand what constitutes bullying and what does not.*

If you are a manager, you are expected to manage, and part of managing is to correct deficiencies and attitudes. As there are ways and means of bullying, there are ways and means of positively motivating, managing, leading and correcting deficiencies and attitudes. While this is beyond the scope of this book, there is ample work done on this, and whether through your employer or on your own you should educate yourself on how to get things done without having to bully.

3. *Know your rights, and exercise them.*

Being bullied is no excuse to be a bully. If bullying is the only way to either survive or get ahead in your organization you should seriously think about making a change. Ultimately you will get caught and have to face the consequences of your behaviors and actions, which could include facing criminal and/or civil charges.

4. *Understand the devastating impact that bullying can have on the individual, the family unit, the organization and the community.*

I believe that everyone can and should be able to relate to this, as at some point in everyone's life they have been a target and/or a bystander, and/or have had someone close to them be a target. By personalizing the impact of bullying, you are better able to conclude that you have to change.

5. *Don't deal with it alone; seek the advice and help of others.*

If you can identify someone in your organization who is a role model who survives and thrives without being a bully, go to that person and ask his or her advice. Other options are to seek the help of a career coach or psychologist. Many organizations will sponsor this. If they do not, it is a worthwhile investment you should make.

6. *Reach out to those you have bullied and apologize.*
Indicate to them that you genuinely want to change and that you want their help by calling you on situations when you cross the line.

7. *Become a role model of someone who survives and thrives without being a bully.*
I encourage bullies to seek redemption; the prerequisite to this is caring. If you don't care for your fellow human being you will have great difficulty in changing your behaviors. Nelson Mandela, in his *Long Walk to Freedom,* put it so well when he wrote, "No one is born hating another person because of the colour of his skin, or his background, or his religion. People must learn to hate, and if they can learn to hate, they can be taught to love, for love comes more naturally to the human heart than its opposite."

Interdependence—
Advice to Families and Friends

"The fundamental law of human beings is
interdependence. A person is a person
through other persons."

—Archbishop Desmond Tutu

When someone is being bullied, you as family member or close friend will know something is wrong based on changes in behaviors, attitudes, physical and mental health.

As I indicate in the chapter "Overcoming It--Advice to the Bullied" people react to bullying in different ways. Some just let it happen, others get angry and retaliate, some become bullies and take out their anger on others (often their families), and others revert to extreme measures such as seriously injuring or killing the people that they feel are responsible for them being bullied. And for others, the only way out is to commit (or attempt) suicide.

Also, I indicate in the same section that it is my belief that people who are being bullied can do something about it in a positive and safe way. Family and/or close friends are in the best position to help.

- Avoiding activities, places or feelings

- Instability or outbursts of anger

- Loss of interest in activities or life in general

- Substance abuse

- Depression
- Guilt, shame or self blame
- Mistrust
- Physical aches and pains

When you notice a combination of these symptoms, it is likely that the person you are close to is dealing with an issue and feels alone, shamed and afraid.

If someone close to you is being bullied I offer the following on what to do (and not do).

1. Make an intervention.

   I advise people who are being targeted not to deal with the issue alone. Ask them directly what is going on and explain why you are asking. Let them talk it through, don't evaluate; actively listen by asking questions to clarify.

2. Give them this book to read.

   Knowing what bullying is and how to effectively deal with it in a safe way is essential. But what is as important is that they need to know, as the proud parent who wrote me the letter included in the introduction, that they are not alone. What they are going through happens to many people.

3. Help them build a strong "Sense of Self".

   They are dwelling on the negatives. You can shift how they feel about themselves by accentuating the positives, the good qualities they have, their accomplishments, their roles at home and in the community. Encourage them to exercise and have the right diet. These are important factors in building a strong sense of self.

4. Guide them on avoiding falling into The Bully's Trap.

   The bully wants to wear the target down to the point where the bullying affects their performance, attendance and attitude. Encourage the bullied to not allow this to happen and focus on excelling, keep their anger in check, and avoid getting sucked into a confrontation with the bully.

5. Don't advise them to get out.

The majority of people who are bullied quit because they believe it is the only way to stop the bullying. Leaving an organization is an option, but it should not be the first one.

Seeking Professional Help

If you believe that the bullied family member or friend could be of danger to himself or others, insist that he seek professional help. If he refuses this, you need to advise his employer so that they are aware that there is a risk, and they can force an intervention. Similarly if you see a significant deterioration in his physical and or mental health, professional help should be sought.

The Unthinkable

The sad reality is that bullying is a factor in suicides or attempted suicides. If bullying is a factor in a family member's suicide or attempted suicide, you should hold the bully and the organization accountable by seeking a criminal charge and/or filing a civil suit against them.

The other sad reality is that bullying is a factor when an employee causes serious harm, including killing others. If bullying is a factor, if a family member or close friend goes to this extreme, the bully and the organization has to bear some of the responsibly, because of the bullying and not preventing the outcome by being aware of the warning signs. You must be the advocate of this.

Advice on Whistle-blowing

Consider how the course of history could have been so different if people in the know reported wrongdoing. Countries and organizations put themselves at huge risk if they have cultures where people are afraid to report wrongdoing. Sadly this is the case in all too many organizations. There is rarely a day where wrongdoing is exposed in the media that damages the brand and reputation of organizations.

Advice to Organizations

Organizations must take the lead on this, first by ensuring they do not have a culture of fear and second by implementing an internal reporting system. The following is recommended:

1. There should be an independent reporting mechanism utilizing an external independent third party. This third party should communicate any reported wrong doing to two different people in the organization.

2. The policy should state that information provided must be clear, truthful and made in good faith.

3. The policy should state clearly what "good faith" means. It doesn't mean that one is always right, just that one honestly thinks one is right or that one honestly thinks there is a valid issue that needs to be reviewed by someone with the skills and knowledge to do so.

4. The policy should ask for the who, what, when, where
   and why—who is involved, what action/non-action is it
   that the whistleblower thinks is wrong, where and when
   did the perceived wrong doing occur, who witnessed the
   behavior, and why does the whistleblower think it is wrong.
   Supporting documentation should be requested. The
   request for such details will assist in the investigation and
   will help to discourage false, frivolous or bad faith claims.

5. Confidentiality is to be guaranteed. No attempt to discover
   the identity of a whistleblower should be made. The policy
   should encourage the giving of the whistleblower's name
   as it will make the investigation easier and more effective.
   If the name is given, then an assurance of non-disclosure
   of the name should be provided to the extent possible. It is
   fair for the policy to advise that failure to provide a name
   or details of the alleged wrongdoing may compromise the
   organization's ability to investigate.

6. A strict non-retaliation policy must be stated, adhered
   to and enforced. It is certainly arguable that if people "in
   the know" have sufficient protection against retaliation,
   certain situations would not have occurred.

7. All reported matters should be investigated.

8. If the whistleblower is known, then providing an update
   on the investigation may be useful, while making it clear
   that confidentiality may restrict the disclosure of details
   of the investigation to the whistleblower. The point is to
   address the concern of the whistleblower that something
   is being done to investigate the wrongdoing reported,
   otherwise the whistleblower may take their concerns to
   the media or another third party.

9. In reviewing reports, the analysis should proceed on the
   assumption that the report was made in good faith, unless
   there is clear evidence to rebut that assumption. Note

that this does not mean that there is an assumption that the report is true, which must be determined based on the investigation.

10. Incorporate into your organization's culture the knowledge that wrongdoing will not be condoned and that everyone has a duty to report any suspected wrongdoing to a supervisor or through the organization's independent whistleblower program. Part of this process will be to ensure that the whistleblower program is publicized. One company took pride that there had never been a report under its whistleblower program only to learn that most employees were unaware of it.

11. Senior management support for the reporting of wrongdoing and the correction of proven wrongdoing has to be stated clearly and unequivocally, and to be seen as real in both word and deed.

Advice to Employees

If your employer has an internal reporting system similar to what is recommended above, and you are comfortable that the system has integrity, follow the protocol that is recommended. If you do not feel that confidentiality will be protected and/or there is potential for retaliation, I would advise making a report to the organization's external auditor. When you do this, seek from them a written assurance that confidentiality is protected.

Regardless of how you report, do it in good faith, with clarity, using the facts you have or what you have heard. Don't embellish, assess or be judgmental. You are simply reporting what you believe is wrong. Whenever I assess reports of wrongdoing, I first determine if the person is registering something they dislike vs. something they truly believe is wrong. Finally, if you observe or hear about a wrongdoing, don't become the investigator. The investigation must be the responsibility of the organization. If you conduct it on your own, you could be in danger of being considered a witch hunter.

A Happy Ending—John's Story

John is the CEO of a large manufacturing company established by his Grandparents in 1927. The company now produces private label products for many of the grocery chains across North America. The company is privately held and the family owns the controlling shares. There are six manufacturing facilities, all of which operate as non-union, which is a source of great pride to John and the other family members. Despite having to make some labor adjustments, the company has enjoyed good relations with their employees.

In 2002 John was able to attract Ryan to run the Ajax Plant, their second largest facility. Ryan came with the right pedigree, having spent the bulk of his career in operations with a global packaged goods company. During the extensive interview process, Ryan said all of the right things and impressed John and the others on the selection committee. They thought he was the right fit with values that were consistent with those of the company's. Ryan was the first outsider in the company's history to be brought in at this level.

Although there were some operating parameters and quality standards, John allowed each facility to operate with a lot of autonomy, as he believed that entrepreneurship was a key to getting superior results.

By all metrics, Ryan was doing a great job. Revenues, profitability, quality and service levels all exceeded plans on a consistent basis.

A number of years earlier John introduced a balanced scorecard for the business, and all departments and facilities were measured on the financials, an employee index and a customer index. Every year an employee attitude survey was conducted. Ryan's facility always scored high, although the participation rate was on average around 70 percent, not as high as the other departments and facilities.

In 2006 the company received notice that the Ajax Plant was the target of a union organizing drive.

Given the results of the employee engagement survey conducted only six months before, this action came as a complete surprise. John's initial reaction was to trust Mary, the company's Vice President of Human Resources, and Ryan, and their advice to do everything possible to keep the union out. John, after all, had the perception that a union would make the plant non-competitive, with rising salaries, limited productivity and restrictive work practices. Mary was responsible for developing the plan to keep the union out. She immediately retained a law firm who had a reputation for union avoidance and union busting, a firm she had worked with at her previous employer. Ryan was responsible for all of the activities that were not handled by the labor lawyer.

The plan that Mary developed involved all of the legal tactics that are usually employed, and included a number of tactics that definitely crossed the line. People who were thought to be ringleaders of the drive had their phones monitored, some were even put under surveillance. Through a third party, a senior person in the union was offered a bribe. Managers and supervisors were coached on how to give subtle messages on what the consequences would be if employees signed cards; and when the time came to vote, if they voted to certify.

In an interview with the press, John indicated that the union would make the facility uncompetitive and they would have to relocate. A capacity study was done; and John and others made it known that there was ample capacity in their other facilities to move all of the production. A number of employees were fired with trumped up allegations of wrongdoing that John was not aware of. All new hires were plants to keep Ryan informed of who was doing what. Each time they came to Ryan with information they received under the table cash. Employees were pitted against employees, and emotions ran high. The legal and surveillance bills went into the hundreds of thousands of dollars.

Throughout all of this, Ryan was in his element; every time he spoke to John he said, "We are going to win, those bastards don't know who they are dealing with."

John kept his Board of Directors apprised of the situation. At a Board meeting three months into it, one of the three Independent Board members asked John, "Why do the employees there feel they need a third party to represent them?" John indicated that he was perplexed by it. Employees there and at the other facilities had a pay rate and benefits that were slightly ahead of competitors who were unionized; and "we treat them well and with respect, this is something that we measure every year in our employee attitude survey." The Board member then asked John whether there were any indicators of discontent that he had observed during his visit to the facility prior to the union drive. John appeared a bit flushed and answered, "No," which was technically an honest answer, but he failed to mention that he had not visited the facility in two years, and when he did, he did not go beyond the office.

The questions bothered John. He realized that he was not close enough to the operations. All he looked at were the results but not how the results were achieved. He needed more points of reference. John recalled that there were a couple of managers he knew who had recently resigned from the Ajax plant, and he called them and asked them to meet him.

They met the next day, and what the former managers told John confirmed John's worst fears. From the time Ryan took over the facility it was run like a dictatorship. Ryan bullied the managers, who in turn bullied the supervisors who bullied the rank and file. Performance was achieved through harassment, threats and fear. Specific examples were given which were appalling to John. "Why didn't you come to me with this?" John asked. The response that came back was, "Ryan would ruin us if he ever found out, and everyone who works there shares this concern." John cited the employee engagement survey results to which the former managers said: Employees don't trust it; and if the results came back negative, Ryan would go on a witch-hunt and punish those who did not play along."

The former managers recommended to John that he review things like the turnover rate, absentee records, number of people who have been on stress leave, lack of comments made on the engagement surveys, and the fact that most employees, including them, were afraid to do an exit interview. They also suggested that John check out the relationship that Ryan had with the companies that Ryan had given the contracts to when the company decided to engage a third party for janitorial and maintenance activities. "You may find they are related to Ryan's wife," one of them said.

After this meeting John contacted Mary and asked her to investigate what the former managers had conveyed; and he wanted to meet with her the next day to review. The next day Mary reported to John that the turnover at the plant ran on average 12 percent for production and distribution employees for the last five years, and an astounding 30 percent for managers and supervisors. The absentee rate was significantly higher at Ajax than at the other facilities. Applications for stress leaves were high, but in most cases challenged by the insurance provider at the request of the plant human resource manager. Mary also indicated that accidents were usually covered up; and anyone with a lost time accident usually went on salary continuation to protect their experience ratings. On the relationship with the third party providers, Mary said she had heard rumours to this effect, but she did not follow up because she was afraid of Ryan as well. "What else do you know?" John asked. Mary admitted that she was aware that there were problems, but had no idea that it was as bad as it was. "Why didn't you come to me?" John asked. Mary responded by saying that the engagement surveys did not validate what she was hearing. "Well obviously the surveys are not worth the paper they were written on." John reacted in exasperation.

All of this was a rude awakening for John. He felt frustrated with himself, betrayed, and seriously questioned whether he was now equipped to fix everything that was wrong. He also felt if he was so out of the loop regarding the Ajax plant, how different would he find the situation at the other facilities?

A meeting of the Board was called, and John laid out the whole situation to them with a plan. First, however, he volunteered to resign if the Board lost confidence in him and said if they did, he would completely understand. The Board gave John the vote of confidence with the qualifier that he needed to take a more hands-on approach in running the company. The Board also unanimously agreed with the plan John had developed.

The first step was to deal with Ryan. John confronted him with what he heard. While Ryan vehemently defended what he referred to as his "aggressive management style," citing the consistent results he had delivered, proving that it works. He could not deny that his brother-in-law owned the outside contractors, and he had not declared a conflict of interest. John asked for and received his resignation. John also sought and received Mary's resignation.

John then met with the President of the union and indicated that the company had put an immediate stop to the actions to avoid the Ajax plant from becoming certified, and would agree to have an employee vote on whether they wanted representation. Further he indicated that he wanted to meet with the employees as a group to let them know that if they elected to be represented, the company would respect their decision; and he would retract the comments and threats to close the plant; and declare that in his view the plant was a solid performer and could continue to be if it were unionized.

A vote was conducted two weeks later and the employees voted to become represented by a high margin. A first agreement was negotiated in record time, and as the wages and benefits were already a bit ahead of the unionized competitors, the company and the union agreed to an incentive program that rewarded productivity, quality and service level targets.

Concurrently a consulting firm was hired to do a thorough cultural assessment of the organization and report back with recommendations within a month's time. The primary objective the company wanted to achieve was to gain the trust of the employees at all of their facilities. John received the report a month later and followed all of the recommendations made in the report with one exception, which was to continue to do an engagement survey. His rationale for this was they had done this over the years and it failed to reveal how employees felt, because, if employees do not trust leadership, they will not trust any mechanism to gauge attitudes. "From now on we are going to hear directly from our employees because they will not be afraid to express their feelings, concerns or ideas," he declared.

The result of going through all this proved very beneficial to the company. Not only did it survive the economic downturn, it prospered. The Ajax plant became the number one performer and all of the other facilities exceeded their targets. The company grew during this period, adding staff. Turnover, absenteeism, and accidents all decreased dramatically. Employees at all of the facilities enjoyed compensation that well exceeded the market because of the incentive program first introduced as a result of the first agreement with Ajax. The program was at Ajax. The program was also implemented at the other facilities. The company enjoyed a great relationship with the union and, as John indicated to the union President, they were "not at all concerned about our other plants being unionized because we are going to make sure they never feel that they need a third party to represent them." The other five facilities and one they added since are non-union.

Attitude or engagement surveys are not conducted. Instead quarterly town hall type meetings are held with all shifts in all facilities. John attends each and every one, communicates results and plans going forward, and opens the meetings for questions and comments. Today, based on the honest exchanges that take place, there does not appear to be a lack of trust.

Investor's Business Daily spent years analyzing leaders and successful people in all walks of life; and they identified ten traits. John's story is an excellent example of their tenth point, which is: "Be Honest and Dependable; Take Responsibility." They point out the key is how well you work with your organization to regain trust. The tips they give are: "bite the bullet, take control, make it right, avoid pitfalls, look through another lens, encourage honesty, solve problems faster, set the standard and move on." John, using his value system and his intuition as a leader, followed all of these tips, and then some.

Employee Activists—
Forcing a Cultural Transformation

"It is possible for a single individual to defy the
whole might of an unjust empire to save his honour,
his religion, his soul, and lay the foundation
for that empire's fall or its regeneration."

—Mahatma Gandhi

The closing case study, "A Happy Ending—John's Story,"
outlines how a positive cultural change was forced because
of a union-organizing drive. This is a rare exception, as organizing
drives are vigorously fought by employers and usually make an
already bad situation worse.

As I argue in this book, for bullying to stop it requires an
organizational transformation. Hopefully leaders will see the
benefit and logic of my argument and initiate the change. Given
the entrenched attitudes that exist, I would not bank on it.

"It is possible for a single individual to defy the whole might of
an unjust empire to save his honour, his religion, his soul, and lay
the foundation for that empire's fall or it's regeneration." These
powerful words by Gandhi are a clarion call to all who work in
toxic cultures. Just as shareholder activists can force a shift in
strategy, the composition of the board, or a change in leadership,
employees, as key, stakeholders can force a change in culture.

Bullying in the workplace puts the organization at risk, and
the impacts are enormous.

The International Federation of Accountants at the United
Nations Conference on Trade Development in 2010 identified

"positioning risk management as a key board responsibility" and concluded that "Governance is more than having the right structures, regulation and principles in place—it is about ensuring that the right behaviors and processes are in place."

Employees are in the best position to ensure the board is made aware of the risk.

A first step is engaging others in the organization who share your concern, and whom you absolutely trust. Ideally this group is representative of a cross section of the organization.

The following is an example, which illustrates how your concerns could be framed.

Statement of Claim

1. We are a group of (X) employees, representing a cross section of the company who are concerned that the toxic culture that exists poses a risk to the organization and all of its stakeholders.

2. We are bringing our concerns forward so that you can ensure that the right behaviors and processes are in place.

3. Our intention and expectation is that the bullying stop.

4. The following outlines recent examples of bullying: (list the examples and provide documentation, e.g. emails, comments on a blog or other social media, video or sound recordings)

5. We recommend the following:

   • an investigation of the examples we have provided

   • a cultural audit (here you can provide a copy of "Conducting a Workplace Assessment—Determining an At Risk Position")

   • appropriate action to ensure the bullying stops

6. We have brought this matter to your attention in good faith and assume no attempt will be made to identify the source of this action, i.e. a "Witch Hunt," and no retaliatory action will be taken.

7. If you, in conducting the investigation, have questions of us, they can be forwarded to (recommend obtaining a safe P.O. Box that is difficult to trace).

The statement of claim should be sent by registered post to either the head of human resources or the organization's lawyer, with a copy to the Chair of Audit of the board.

If after sixty days there is no change in behaviors, a follow up should be sent indicating that the situation has not changed (or has gotten worse). In this you should request a response to the P.O. Box outlining the organization's position on the matter.

If after thirty days no response is provided, you should send a letter indicating that you will be exposing the situation to major shareholders or the media.

If you or others suspect a "witch hunt" or retaliation, seek immediate legal advice.

And in conclusion

The following is the commencement address that I gave to graduates of a College of Applied Arts and Technology in Ontario, Canada, in June of 2011.

> *By many standards I have lived a charmed and successful life. Like everyone, there have been setbacks, challenges and personal tragedies, all of which helped define who I am and what I stand for.*
>
> *Six years ago, being diagnosed with leukemia and given a life sentence was one of those challenges.*

Were it not for a miracle drug which turned what was a fatal condition to a chronic one, I would be dead today. This experience forced me to reflect on the reason for being, and discovering that notwithstanding the successes enjoyed, there was a void which was, really having made a difference. What was missing was a lack of purpose.

Today my life is full of purpose, reflected in part through my philanthropy, but to a greater extent it is putting a stop to what I believe to be an epidemic—bullying in the workplace.

There is no need for me to explain to you what bullying is and the devastating impact it has other than to say bullying in schools shares many of the characteristics with bullying in the work place. As there are similarities there are differences, the most significant being the ways and means are more subtle and there are fewer avenues for people to exit from the situation.

Bullies are masters of deflection, usually they discredit their targets to the point the target become the villain. They "kiss up and kick down." Because they are viewed as high performers they are treated like heroes who garner more credibility than the target.

The mighty have fallen because of organizational cultures that condone and encourage bullying.

In analyzing the demise of Enron, AIG, Lehmann Bothers, and the list goes on, they all had a common characteristic, which was their CEO's were also CBO's—Chief Bullying Officer's.

The global financial meltdown could have been avoided had people who were in the know, reported wrongdoings. They did not, largely for fear of being retaliated against. In most cases whistleblowers are viewed as traitors and subject to bullying as punishment for their treason.

Bullying has always occurred, however it shames me to say that my generation has systematically, largely because of greed, created dictatorial leadership, where fear has become a substitute for motivation and positive leadership.

We have allowed tyranny and domination to dictate the culture in which to work.

This is the sad legacy that my generation leaves to you.

Many have expressed, stopping this epidemic is "mission impossible."

For us it is not a question of "Can it be stopped?" It is an assertion: "It must be stopped." For it to be eliminated, everyone has a role to play.

Everyone graduating today will, at some point in your career, become a bully, and/or be bullied and/or be a bystander.

If history is any indicator only a small percent of you will become defenders of those who are bullied.

Where there has been genocide, which is the most extreme form of bullying, only a small percent of the population became witness and defenders of those who were targeted. Had the small percent been a mere ten percent, the course of history would have had a different outcome.

The revolutions in the Middle East, with the over throw of tyranny is proof positive that the course of history can be changed, and serves as an inspiration to have the small percent become ten percent.

Over your careers you will be faced with choices. The most difficult ones for you will be whether or not to be a witness and defender of those who are targeted, becoming part of the ten percent.

This choice involves risk, and requires courage. The risks of being a witness and defender are obvious. However, in making the risk assessment, consider the risk of not being that witness and defender. Consider never having to say,

- *I could have prevented the ruin of my coworker's career. Consider never having to say,*
- *I could have prevented the breakup of a family unit. Consider never having to say,*
- *I could have helped avoid the demise of an organization. Consider never having to say,*
- *I could have prevented a suicide or attempted suicide. Consider never having to say,*
- *I could have prevented someone going postal and killing others.*

Mahatma Gandhi put it so well when he declared, "It is possible for a single individual to defy the whole might of an unjust empire to save his honour, his religion, his soul, and lay the foundation for that empire's fall or its regeneration."

As this choice involves risk, it also yields rewards, the greatest of which is strengthening your sense of self, helping to make right what is wrong and making the lives of others free and safe from the ravages of tyranny.

By becoming part of that ten percent, you can change the course of history.

Author's Note

Organizational transformation will be the focus of my next book. My hope is to tell the stories of where there have been successful transformations, the resulting impacts and how the change occurred. To help me on this, I encourage those who have experienced this kind of positive change to send me your story at andrew@bullyingattheworkplace.com

Acknowledgments

I doubt that any book can be written in isolation. For those who try shortchange themselves and more importantly the reader. Writers need support, encouragement, and critical input. This I received in spades and am forever grateful.

My partner Lee Wells helped me through the periods of self doubt (there were many) and boosted my self confidence. Eleanor Pope, who has been my Executive Assistant for fifteen years (which says something about both of us), has kept me focused, on track, and put some semblance of order in my scattered thoughts, sentences, and paragraphs (for those who know me, not an insignificant accomplishment).

Giving an author critical input is not an easy task, particularly if there is friendship involved—you want to be honest, but you also don't want to hurt feelings. Virginia Cirocco, Catherine Faas, Jennifer Grant, Karen Gruson, Velvet and John Haney, Ryan Jackson, Keith Juriansz, Catherine Labrosse, Susan McClelland, Bobbi Reinholdt, Dr. Tom Reynolds, Maureen Ryan, and Paris Vlahovic all gave me the much needed critical, direct feedback with such kindness it fostered even better relationships.

The research provided by Glenn Pound in the early stages of the book helped me put the issue of bullying into context.

Finally to all of the people interviewed for this book, their stories raised my level of indignation on what all too many people have to endure every day, this has increased my passion and resolve to do what I can to stop bullying from occurring in the workplace.

Index

Uganda, 223
UK Telegraph, 132
United Nations (UN), 179, 247
United Nations Conference on Trade Development (UNCTAD), 247
United States of America (USA), 177
United States National Crime Prevention Council, 111
University of Southern California, 177
University of Toronto, 1
University of Virginia Literacy magazine,179
University of Virginia, 179
US (Postal Service) team, 105
US Department of Justice, 7
US Anti-doping Agency (USADA), 106
US Equal Employment Opportunity Commission (EEOC), 154
US National Institute for Occupational Safety and Health, 178
Vancouver, 137, 165, 168
Vancouver Q Hall of Fame, 137
Vanity Fair, 70
Vatican Bank, 50
Virginia Quarterly Review, 179
Vlahovic, Paris, 1, 253

Wall Street, 69
Wall Street Journal, 137
Watergate, 42
Watkins, Sharron, 34
Wauthier, Pierre, 68, 122
Wayne State University, 175
Weimaraner, 9
Western Canada, 149
Wells, Lee John, 253
Wilde, Oscar, 31
Wilson, Woodrow, 214
Windsor, 97
WorldCom, 67
Yale University, 41
YouTube, 181
Xtra, 138
Zaccerdelli, Giuliano, 44
Zeiwing, David, 68
Zimbardo, Philip, Dr., PH.D, 40
Zurich Insurance Company, 68, 122

Endnotes

Grimme, Sheryl and Don. "'Violence in the Workplace - The Realities and the Options." *Business Know How.*
Petrecca, Laura. "Bullying by the boss is common but hard to fix." *USA Today,* December 28, 2010.

Part One
WINFIELD, NICOLE. "Pope Blasts Vatican Administration, Lists Its Sins in Christmas Greeting." The Associated Press, December 22, 2014. http://www.theglobeandmail.com/news/world/pope-blasts-vatican-administration-lists-its-sins-in-christmas-greeting/article22176415/
Bronskill, Jim, and Joan Bryden. "Ex-staffers bristle at Ouimet's 'Cadillac package'." *Canadian Press,* March 09, 2011.
Milgram, Stanley. Harper's Magazine. "The Perils of Obedience." *Abridged and adapted from Obedience to Authority,* December 1973. The four R's (doing the RIGHT things, the RIGHT way, by the RIGHT people at the RIGHT time.) *Adaption from* 4R-CE. http://www.4r-ce.com/business-needs/
Payton, Laura and Crawford, Alison. "7 issues facing the RCMP commissioner." *CBC News,* October 27, 2011. http://www.cbc.ca/news/politics/story/2011/10/27/pol-list-rcmp-issues-comissioner.html.
Greenberg, Allan. *The Rise and Fall of Bear Stearns.* Simon & Schuster, 2010. Alan
Fraser, Sheila. The Public Sector Integrity Commissioner of Canada - Report of the Auditor-General's, "Office of

the Auditor General of Canada." December 14, 2010. http:// www.oag-bvg.gc.ca

Davis, Nick. "Sean Hoare knew how destructive the News of the World could be." *The Guardian,* July 18, 2011.

The Diagnostic and Statistical Manual of Mental Disorders IV Festinger, L., ed. Stanford, CA: Stanford University Press, 1957. s.v.

"A theory of cognitive dissonance."

Skelton, Chad, and Andrea Woo. "More than 200 B.C. RCMP employees now on sick leave." *Vancouver Sun,* June 24, 2010. *Paul Palango, Dispersing the Fog: Inside the Secret World of Ottawa and the RCMP, (Key Porter Books, 2008),* 255.

Skelton, Chad. "Six in 10 B.C. RCMP staff have thought about quitting." *Vancouver Sun,* May 12, 2010.

"RESTORING THE HONOR OF THE RCMP." *ADDRESSING PROBLEMS IN THE ADMINISTRATION OF THE RCMP'S PENSION AND INSURANCE PLANS.* (December 2007):39th

Parliament, 2nd session, 11and 117.

MacCharles, Tonda. "Revolt in senior ranks spurs probe of RCMP chief." *toronto star,* July 28, 2010. www.rcmp-grc.gc.ca/index-eng.htm

"Accountancy Summit on Corporate Governance Reform Looks Beyond the Global Financial Crisis." (Oct 2010). http:// www.ifac.org/news-events/2010-10/accountancy- summit-corporate-governance-reform-looks-beyond-global-financial-cri.

Charan, Ram. *Owning Up.* Jossey-Bass, 2009.

Charan, Ram. *Boards That Deliver.* Jossey-Bass, 2005.

McDonald, Lawrence G. *A Colossal Failure of Common Sense.* Crown Business, 2010.

Lewis, Michael. "The Man Who Crashed the World." *Vanity Fair,* August 2009. http://www.vanityfair.com/politics/features/2009/08/aig200908

Taibbi

Tiabbi, Matt. "How Wall Street Is Using the Bailout to Stage a Revolution." *Rolling Stone magazine,* April 02, 2009. http://www.rollingstone.com/politics/news/how-wall-street-is-using-the- bailout-to-stage-a-revolution-20090402

Part Two

"The Dignity at work Compign," http://dignityatwork.org

Ewing, Jack. "Suicide Draw's Attention to a Top Banker's Tough Tactics", New York Times, August 31, 2013.

Willsher, Kim. "Orange France Investigates Second Wave of Suicides". http://www.theguardian.com, March 19, 2014

Beale, David and Helge Hoel. "Workplace bullying, industrial relations and the challenge for management in Britain and Sweden." *European Journal of Industrial Relations* 16(2), 101— 118;

Sutton, Robert. Good Boss, Bad Boss. New York: Business Plus, 2010.

Kwoh, Leslie. "A Silence That Hangs Over CEO's." *The Wall Street Journal,* July 25, 2012. http://online.wsj.com/article/SB10000872396390044329540457754704370537461 0.html

"Southern Poverty Law Center," http://www.splcenter.org/.

Casserly, Meghan. "When Snitches Get Stitches." *Physical Violence As Workplace Retaliation On The Rise,* September 21, 2012.

Grant, Jaime M., Lisa A. Mottet, and Justin Tanis. "Injustice at Every Turn." *A Report of the National Transgender Discrimination Survey.* (2011): 9.

UK and National Work Advice Line "International Communications Research," http://www. icrsurvey.com/

Leymann, Heinz. "The Content and Development of Mobbing at Work." *European Journal of Work & Organizational Psychology.* 1996, 5 (2), 165-184.

Bjorkqvist, Kaj, Osterma, Karin, and Hjelt-Back, Monika. "Aggression Among University Employees." *Aggressive Behavior.* (1994): 173-184.

Porath, Christine, and Christine Pearson. "How Toxic Colleagues Corrode Performance." *Harvard Business Review,* April 2009.

Porath, Christine, and Christine Pearson. *The Cost Of Bad Behavior.* 2009.

Kinder, Andrew and Cooper, Cary L The cost of suicide and sudden death within an organization (UK); Death Studies 33: 411-419, 2009.

Part Three
Robert Hare http://www.hare.org

Part Four
Fadiman, Clifton. *The American Treasury.* New York : Harper, 1955 Sutton, Robert. *Good Boss, Bad Boss.* New York: Business Plus,
2010.

Appendices
Blair, Julie. "New Breed of Bullies Torment Their Peers on the Internet." 22 *Education Week 6,* February 05, 2003. http://web4.epnet.com Kabay, M.E. "Anonymity and Pseudonymity in Cyberspace: Deindividuation, Incivility and Lawlessness Versus Freedom and Privacy." *Ann. Conf European Inst. For Computer Antivirus Research.* (1998).

(adapted from, Case Study: Cyber-bullying and Free Speech, the Knight Foundation)